What God Has Joined Together

Studies for Christian Couples

Jesus Loves Families Series

Edited by
Joshua L. Pappas

What God Has Joined Together: Studies for Christian Couples

Published by Cypress Publications

Copyright © 2025 by Heritage Christian University Press

Manufactured in the United States of America

Cataloging-in-Publication Data

What God has joined together: studies for Christian couples / edited by Joshua L. Pappas

Jesus loves families series

p. cm.

Includes scripture index.

ISBN 979-8-89733-007-2 (pbk.) 979-8-89733-008-9 (ebook)

1. Marriage—Religious aspects—Christianity. 2. Christian life—Study and teaching I. Editor. II. Title. II. Series.

248.844—dc20

Cover design by Brittany Vander Maas.

For information:

Cypress Publications
3625 Helton Drive
PO Box HCU
Florence, AL 35630

www.hcu.edu/publications

Contents

Preface

In the church I serve, our leadership team recognized a need to emphasize marriage and family ministry for the sake of building up our couples and helping them raise their children to be faithful followers of Jesus. There are few needs a church can focus on that are more important and few efforts more likely to bear good fruit in service to the King.

We started a Marriage Ministry eNewsletter that we publish once a quarter, through which we share news, publish member anniversaries, share helpful articles, and promote already available resources (like good books, podcasts, etc.) that will help our couples flourish spiritually and physically. We committed to hosting regular marriage seminars and workshops, having already supported a regional marriage retreat that several of our couples attend annually. We also formed a couples' class (that meets each Lord's Day) and began looking for good teaching materials.

There is good material our brothers and sisters in the churches of Christ have produced, but not nearly enough of it. I felt the need to try to add something that will be of great value to our churches as well as to individual Christian couples seeking teaching resources to help them strengthen their marriages. That felt need was the genesis of this project, of which my fellow writers and I hope the Lord will bless us to produce four volumes in a series called *Jesus Loves Families*. This is the first volume, and I pray our Lord will use it widely and effectively. May generations be blessed by the writings in this book.

This study draws from the skills of a cross-section of capable ministers and teachers from across America. All proceeds from the sale of the books in this series will go to Heritage Christian University, my alma mater, and one of the greatest places on earth to learn to communicate the gospel effectively. May God continue to bless HCU in every way. Over half of the contributing authors in this volume are HCU alumni. I trust all our readers will appreciate the wisdom, knowledge, and skill with which each has handled his assigned subject. To God alone be the glory!

I want to express my sincere gratitude to each contributing writer, some of whom made a considerable sacrifice of time out of their already busy schedules to help. I also want to speak to you, brothers, directly and say, I am impressed with the work you have done for this project. I have been edified by reading and rereading your work during the editing process. Any mistakes that may yet remain in the text are mine, not theirs. Together, we dedicate this volume to our Savior, without Whom we would be dead and hopeless, but in Whose love we have all been redeemed from sin, blessed with lives of meaningful and fulfilling service, despite the hardships through which He has, and we trust always will, walked with us, and Whom we each long to see in glory with resurrected eyes. Lord Jesus, our King, we humbly submit ourselves to You as Your grateful servants and pray with all our hearts that You will judge our work worthy and cause much good to result from its circulation. Maranatha!

The Editor
May 23, 2025

The Traditional Wedding Vows

These are a version of the old traditional wedding vows that originated from the medieval Sarum Rite, and which spread throughout the English-speaking world, globally, through various Ministers' Manuals.

The Groom's Vow

I, *groom*, take thee, *bride*, to my wedded wife, to have and to hold from this day forward, for better or for worse, for richer or for poorer, in sickness and in health, to love and to cherish, till death do us part, according to God's holy ordinance; and thereto I plight thee my troth.

Bride's Vow

I, *bride*, take thee, *groom*, to my wedded husband, to have and to hold from this day forward, for better or for worse, for richer or for poorer, in sickness and in health, to love, cherish, and to obey, till death do us part, according to God's holy ordinance; and thereto I give thee my troth.

Ring Exchange

With this ring I thee wed, with my body I thee worship, and with all my worldly goods I thee endow: In the Name of the Father, and of the Son, and of the Holy Ghost. Amen.

Minister's Pronouncement

Forasmuch as *groom* and *bride* have consented together in holy wedlock, and have witnessed the same before God and this company, and thereto have given and pledged their troth either to the other, and have declared the same by the giving and receiving of a ring, and by joining of hands; I pronounce that they be man and wife together, In the Name of the Father, and of the Son, and of the Holy Ghost. What therefore God hath joined together, let not man put asunder. Amen.

Chapter 1

Holy Matrimony

Understanding Marriage and the Biblical Roles of Husband and Wife

Joshua Pappas

Focus Passage

Then the LORD God said, "It is not good that the man should be alone; I will make him a helper fit for him." Now out of the ground the LORD God had formed every beast of the field and every bird of the heavens and brought them to the man to see what he would call them. And whatever the man called every living creature, that was its name. The man gave names to all livestock and to the birds of the heavens and to every beast of the field. But for Adam there was not found a helper fit for him. So the LORD God caused a deep sleep to fall upon the man, and while he slept took one of his ribs and closed up its place with flesh. And the rib that the LORD God had taken from the man he made into a woman and brought her to the man. Then the man said,

"This at last is bone of my bones
and flesh of my flesh;
she shall be called Woman,

because she was taken out of Man."

Therefore a man shall leave his father and his mother and hold fast to his wife, and they shall become one flesh. And the man and his wife were both naked and were not ashamed (Gen 2:18–25).[i]

One Main Thing

God created humankind in His own image, both male and female. He drew the two to Himself and performed the original wedding ceremony and placed them in their paradise garden home. How beautiful! While we know that in the resurrection we will "neither marry nor [be] given in marriage" (Matt 22:30), in this life we know little about being human that doesn't flow from and isn't built on the foundation of marriage. The old playground rhyme, "First comes love, then comes marriage, then comes the baby carriage," altered to include whatever boy's name was being accused of liking a girl, is the order of life in all normal circumstances. And it is very good! We used to learn some of life's most enduring lessons on the playground. I hope today's children still can.

Introduction

I wish that everyone had a "model Christian marriage" to look up to while growing up. For me, it was my paternal grandparents. Victor and Betty Jean Pappas were happily married for over 50 years before my grandmother's passing. Over the years of my childhood and into early adulthood, I was blessed to witness their eager embrace of the biblical roles of husband and wife while, for many years, both worked outside the home in stressful jobs. They vocally kept their love for Jesus as the center of everything in their lives. They kissed each other almost as much as they kissed on their grandchildren. My "Grandmama" was one of the best cooks who has ever lived, and having grown up during the Great Depression, she was deeply concerned that her grandchildren eat and not be too skinny—and with her cooking, it wasn't a hard sell! They spoke tenderly to each other and called each other pet names. I never saw or heard them argue or fight. Asking my father about this, he assured me they had disagreements over the years, but always took them to their bedroom so that they could work through them in private and always present a united front to my uncle and him. They exemplified the "one flesh" aspect of marriage beautifully, and while I have failed to live up to their example in some ways (not to mention Jesus's perfect example), I have modeled the way I've tried to live with my wife after their fine example, and I thank God for it. May we all give similar examples to our children and grand-children!

Going Deeper

Marriage is God's institution for His glory and our benefit. He has defined it, and no one has the right to change it. Marriage is between one man and one woman for life.[ii] While passages like Deuteronomy 24:1–4; Matthew 5:31–32, 19:1–9, and 1 Corinthians 7:10–16 teach about the possibility or forbiddance of remarriage after a divorce, God's desire is that His people never divorce at all. He hates divorce (Mal 2:13–16). The biblical ideal is "What therefore God has joined together, let not man separate" (Matt 19:6).

If you haven't already, read through the traditional

wedding vows in the preface of this book. While the precise statements aren't in the Bible, every word is drawn from its teachings. Regardless of whether you spoke these traditional vows in your ceremony or prepared some sweet promises of your own, marriage is as God has defined it, and if you're married, you owe it to your Maker to keep the promises He has bound husbands and wives to keep. Never forget, marriage didn't start with you. You've been blessed by something God made, and, as many have said, He made it to help you find happiness in life, but He made it to help you be holy more than to be happy. A happy marriage is a holy marriage. Regard your vows and the sweet union they created as sacred (Heb 13:4).

There are essential roles in a biblical marriage. There can be diversity in how we express them, but some things are the husband's role, and others are exclusively the wife's. For instance, the husband is the "head" of the wife and, under Christ (1 Cor 11:3), the leader of his family.

> Paul writes,
>
> Wives, submit to your own husbands, as to the Lord. For the husband is the head of the wife even as Christ is the head of the church, his body, and is himself its Savior. Now as the church submits to Christ, so also wives should submit in everything to their husbands. (Eph 5:22–24).

The original Greek word translated as "head" is "*kephalé*." It's the word for the magnificent structure that sits atop each of our necks, but metaphorically (as Paul uses it in Ephesians 5), it refers to "anything supreme, chief, or prominent."[iii] Many have debated the meaning of this word. As with any word, it may have nuances of meaning, but whatever the nuance, it does mean the man is to be the leader of his household, including his wife. Furthermore, Scripture teaches the husband to love his wife to the point of self-sacrifice (Eph 5:25). The context of Ephesians 5:22–33 (a vital text for understanding marriage) is built upon the example of Christ as husband and church as bride. Righteous leaders are servant-leaders. They do not make fulfilling their own desires their primary goal but see to it that those they lead are provided for, nourished, protected, and guided in the Lord's way (Eph 6:1–4). Holy husbands lay down their lives for their wives and so model the loving leadership of Christ. It's hard not to respect a true servant-leader.

Ephesians 5:22–24 also speaks to the role of the wife. Paul commands Christian wives to "submit" to their own husbands "as to the Lord." The commandment includes both the duty and the extent to which it is to be carried out. The original Greek word translated "submit" is part of a phrase that would literally read something like, "Wives, to your own husbands as to the Lord." It flows from verse 21. Listen to it as the original readers would have heard it without the verse numbers and section headings added by publishers: "Submitting to one another out of reverence for Christ, wives, to your own husbands as to the Lord." Some opponents of the biblical teachings about the roles of husbands and wives like to try to use verse 21 to nullify or limit verse 22. It just shows their ignorance of the original text. The way the passage is worded in Greek, verse 22 highlights how a wife is to obey verse 21, namely by submitting to her husband just as she submits to the Lordship of Christ.

But what does submission mean? Times change, and what once was will come around again (Eccl 1:9), but for much of my lifetime, many have maligned the idea of submission, especially that of a wife to her husband. It doesn't mean she's inferior, less valuable, less intelligent, or any such thing. It means that just as the husband has the responsibility to model Christ for all to see, so she has the responsibility to model the church for all to see. A Christian marriage is a sort of lived-out gospel sermon. Couples will face difficulty raising godly children (one of God's original purposes for marriage, (cf. Gen 1:28, Mal 2:15) if they reject the Christ and church roles of daddy and mama in their household. Trust God's wisdom. All His commands are designed to help us (1 John 5:3). A holy wife gladly submits to her husband's headship in the home as if he were Jesus, even though she knows, perhaps better than anyone else, he's only at best a poor (but hopefully sincere) imitation.

Space will not permit an exhaustive exploration of every duty of husband and wife, but take note of the following. Both husband and wife may work outside the home as needed (Prov 31:13–19), but the primary respon- sibility to provide and protect is the husband's (1 Tim 5:8), and the primary responsibility to nurture small children and maintain an orderly household is the wife's (1 Tim 5:14, Titus 2:3–5). The calling to be a homemaker is the highest possible for a wife and mother and should be honored in the church very highly. The church must return to encouraging our little girls to this calling as preferable to climbing the proverbial corporate ladder. It is the ideal way women bear fruit for the Lord if the Lord allows them to bear children or adopt them (1 Tim 2:15; James 1:27). And never forget, a husband's faithfulness to his calling does not depend on whether his wife is what she should be, and the wife's faithfulness to her God-given role does not depend on whether her husband is a worthy leader. Both husband and wife obey the Scriptures out of loyalty to Christ, regardless of how well (or poorly) their spouse does.

Application

Read through each of these summary applications carefully and take mental note of each. As you read, try to think of specific ways you will employ each admonition in your own life and marriage.

- Recognize marriage as God's creation, designed for His glory and our benefit, between one man and one woman for life. Christians must honor marriage as a sacred covenant, not subject to redefinition by human standards.
- Embrace the distinct roles of husband and wife as outlined in Scripture. Husbands are called to servant-leadership, modeling Christ's sacrificial love for the church, while wives are called to submit to their husbands' leadership as the church submits to Christ.
- Pursue holiness in marriage as the path to true happiness, understanding that a holy marriage aligns with God's design and reflects His relationship with the church.
- View marriage as God's provision for companionship, procreation, and the establishment of a stable foundation for civilization. It serves as a model of Christ's love for the church and a foretaste of eternal intimacy with God.
- Fulfill God-given marital roles out of obedience to Christ, not based on the spouse's

performance. God's commands for husbands and wives are designed for their good and His glory, even in challenging circumstances.

- Recognize parenting and homemaking as high callings, particularly for wives, to raise godly children and maintain an orderly household. The church should encourage young women to value these roles over worldly ambitions.

- Live out marriage as a testimony of Christ's love for the church, demonstrating truth, goodness, and beauty to a fallen world through daily actions, serving as a witness to others of God's design for relationships.

Conclusion

The biblical narrative that ends with the establishment of marriage began with God's observation, "It is not good that the man should be alone; I will make him a helper fit for him" (Gen 2:18). God designed marriage as the solution to loneliness. It is for companionship. It is for procreation (the inability to bear children should be seen as an opportunity to practice "religion that is pure and undefiled" rather than as a curse). It is for the pleasure of a pure sex life. It is to model the beautiful love between Christ and His holy bride, the church. It is to build up the church. It is to establish a solid basis for all civilization. It is between one man and one woman for life, and if you keep your vows, it will be the basis for your generational legacy. It is, when lived out according to Scripture, one of the most wonderful expressions of all that is true, good, and beautiful in our fallen world. When it's holy, it's a little taste of the ecstasy of the intimacy we will all enjoy in the presence of the Lord in the Age to Come. May God bless all our marriages in Christ!

Discussion Questions

1. How can we, as individuals and as the church, uphold and promote the biblical definition of marriage in a culture that often challenges it?

2. What are some practical ways couples can live out their biblical roles in their daily lives, and how can the church support them in embracing these responsibilities?

3. How can couples cultivate holiness in their marriage through spiritual practices, and what challenges might they face in making holiness the foundation of their relationship?

4. How can Christian couples use their marriage to model Christ's love to their children, community, or others, and what impact might this have on those around them?

Endnotes

[i] All Scripture references are from the English Standard Version (ESV) unless otherwise specified.

[ii] While God allowed polygamy to exist before the establishment of the church, it was not His original will as revealed in Genesis 1 and 2. Polygamy came into being through the rebellion of Cain's lineage (Gen 4:19), but quickly spread through all people groups, including, after the Flood, even Abraham and his descendants. God regulated it in the Law of Moses, but through Jesus, returned

His people to His original intent (Matt 19:4). Built on the foundation of Jesus's teachings, the Holy Spirit inspired the apostle Paul to write "But because of the temptation to sexual immorality, each man should have his own wife and each woman her own husband" (1 Cor 7:2). Note the singular possessive pronouns: "each man ... his own," and "each woman ... her own." If a wife is one of multiple, "each" does not have "her own," but rather a shared husband. God no longer accepts polygamy. His plan for the duration of this Christian Age is what He intended from the beginning: One man and one woman for life.

[iii] Larry Pierce, "Outline of Biblical Usage," Blue Letter Bible, accessed May 22, 2025, https://www.bluelet terbible.org/lexicon, (https://www.blueletterbible.org/resources/lexical/overview.cfm), s.v. κεφαλή.

Chapter 2

From This Day Forward

How to Grow Spiritually as a Couple
Marricus D. Ellis

FOCUS PASSAGE:

Wives, subject yourselves to your own husbands, as to the Lord. For the husband is the head of the wife, as Christ also is the head of the church, He Himself being the Savior of the body. But as the church is subject to Christ, so also the wives ought to be to their husbands in everything. Husbands, love your wives, just as Christ also loved the church and gave Himself up for her, so that He might sanctify her, having cleansed her by the washing of water with the word, that He might present to Himself the church in all her glory, having no spot or wrinkle or any such thing; but that she would be holy and blameless. So husbands also ought to love their own wives as their own bodies. He who loves his own wife loves himself; for no one ever hated his own flesh, but nourishes and cherishes it, just as Christ also does the church, because we are parts of His body. For this reason a man shall leave his father and his mother and be joined to his wife, and the two shall become one flesh. This mystery is great; but I am speaking with reference to Christ and the church (Eph 5:22–32).[i]

One Main Thing

Ephesians 5:22–32 is a very interesting passage concerning marriage. In this pericope,[ii] the Apostle Paul seeks to exhort the church at Ephesus on how to have a marriage that reflects the marriage of Christ and the church. He helps us to understand how wives should conduct themselves toward their husbands, and how husbands should conduct themselves toward their wives. What's interesting about this is that the conduct of the husband and the wife is based on Christ and the church. This means that Paul's instruction for marriage for those who are in the church derives from the demonstration of marriage from God toward the Church. Therefore, this passage not only instructs us on how to have a godly marriage, but it also helps us appreciate the union we have with Christ.

Introduction

I remember as a kid hearing my teachers encourage us to grow up, go to college, get married, and have children. This was, and perhaps still is, the "American dream." As a kid, I looked forward to achieving this dream. I looked forward to the wedding day, building a family, and living happily ever after. However, as I reflect, no one really taught me the purpose of marriage or what happens after the vows are spoken and the wedding ceremony ends. No one really taught me what happens "From this day forward." What are we supposed to do? What's the purpose of our union? How can we use this marriage to honor and glorify God?

These are questions that everyone should ask (especially Christians) before entering a covenant with another person. I believe there are many Christian marriages that are struggling today, because they don't know what to do "from this day forward." In this chapter, I want to encourage Christian couples on how to grow spiritually together and how to have a marriage that honors and glorifies God.

Ephesians 5:22–32 is about Paul instructing the church at Ephesus on how to have a marriage like Christ and the church. In this portion of Ephesians, Paul is exhorting the church on how we should behave, based on what God has done for us through Jesus Christ. In chapters 1–3, Paul deals with Christian doctrine and clearly articulates the gospel of Jesus Christ, and how God sent His Son into the world to provide peace and reconciliation between man and God (Eph 2:1–18). In chapters 4–6, Paul shifts from Christian doctrine to Christian duty, and he says, based on what God has done for us through Christ, here is how you should live and conduct your life (Eph 4:1ff). It is within the fabric of Paul's instruction on Christian duty that we find our passage concerning Christian marriage. This passage provides us with valuable instruction regarding the character and conduct of Christian marriage, and it points us to Jesus, who is the foundation and hope for any marriage that seeks to honor and glorify God. Without Him at the center of our marriages, our union is in vain, and our hope for spiritual growth has diminished tremendously.

Going Deeper

At the beginning of chapter 5, Paul begins with the inferential, coordinating conjunction "therefore," which means he is offering a conclusion to the preceding discussion. In chapter 4, Paul begins his exhortation on the Christian's duty, and how we should live our lives according to what God has done for us through Christ. He exhorts the church to "put off" the old man—to get rid of the person you were before coming to Christ. That person died with Christ in baptism (Rom 6:3–4)! We are to "put on" the new man, "which is in the likeness of God and has been created in righteousness, holiness, and truth" (Eph 4:24). It is this "new man," who is in the likeness of God, that Paul has in mind as he begins Chapter 5. He says, "Therefore [because we are new creatures in Christ] be imitators of God, as beloved children" (Eph 5:1). Paul uses the Greek term "μιμηταί" ("*mimetai*") for imitators, which means to impersonate, forge, or copy. Paul says, as children of God, we ought to copy God in every aspect of our lives. That is what the entire chapter is about: imitating God.

Therefore, following this concept of imitation, Paul demonstrates how we should imitate Christ and the church in our marriages. In verse 21, Paul instructs the church to submit to one another in the fear of Christ, but he then brings down the same concept of submission in verse 22 with an instruction to wives specifically. He says, "Wives, be subject to your own husbands, as to the Lord." In the original Greek language, there is no verb here, but the whole structure of the verse depends on the imperative participle in verse 21, which is a mutual submission in reverence to God. So, this text does not isolate nor belittle women in any way, but it is an instruction for how God expects the wife to conduct herself in the family (cf. 1 Cor 11:3, Col 3:18, Titus 2:5, 1 Pet 3:1–2). Francis Foulkes writes in his commentary,

It is significant that throughout this section husbands and wives are reminded of their duties and not their rights. It is important also to read all that is said in this section realizing both that it follows what has been said in verse 21 about mutual submission and that it presupposes what is stated in Galatians 3:28 of the equality in Christ of male and female. In the Christian family, however, as Paul sees it there is order and wives are called to be subject to their husbands."[iii]

If we want to have godly marriages and grow spiritually together, then we must follow God's way. A lesson we can learn here is that it is important for men to lead their families spiritually, as Christ leads all of us. Every instruction in this pericope is based on what Christ does for us; He leads us and guides us spiritually, and as husbands, we should do the same with our wives. We should not be like the first Adam, who, because of fear, hid in the garden (Gen 3:8), but we should be like the second Adam (Christ), who boldly stands up and protects His bride (the church).

This leads us to verses 23 and 24, where Paul gives the basis for the wives' subjection to their husbands, which is that the church is subject to Christ. Paul then shifts to the husbands in verse 25 and instructs men to "LOVE their wives." It has often been said, husbands love your wives, and wives respect your husbands. The Bible doesn't say this verbatim, but the principle is there. If we want to grow spiritually in our marriages, we must take heed to these instructions and "encourage one another to love and good deeds" (Heb 10:24). Oftentimes, the more a husband loves his wife, the more his wife will respect him and vice versa. Paul uses the Greek word "αγαπαω" ("*agapao*") for love here, which means, "warm regard for and interest in another, *esteem,*

affection, regard, love."[iv] When a husband does this, he is
reflecting Christ's love for the church, making it easier for
his wife to honor and respect him. However, there is a
deeper reason a husband loves his wife. Paul lays it out in
verses 26–27. He says,

> so that He might sanctify her, having cleansed her by the
> washing of water with the word, that He might present to
> Himself the church in all her glory, having no spot or
> wrinkle or any such thing; but that she would be holy and
> blameless.

Wow! Can you imagine how different our marriages
would be if all husbands put this into practice? This is what
Christ has done for us, this is why we have salvation,
because Christ sanctified us (Titus 2:14), cleansed us (2 Pet
1:9), washed us with His word (1 Cor 6:11; Titus 3:5; John
15:3, 17:17) so that He might present us to Himself
without spot or blemish. Husbands, are you cleansing your
wives with the word? Are you studying the word together,
are you praying over her, are you demonstrating the love of
Christ, that you might present her spotless? These are
things we must do if we want our marriages to grow spiritually.

Paul closes this pericope by reminding us that husband
and wife are one flesh, and no man hates his own flesh, but
he nourishes it (Eph 5:28–29). He then informs us that all
of this is in reference to Christ and the Church—that this is
what Christ has done and is still doing for us today—loving
us, cleansing us, nourishing us to present us spotless before
the Father. As the Church submits to Him, it is inevitable
that we will grow, because that is His desire for us. To the
couples reading, is this your desire?

Application

- The first thing we can gather from Ephesians 5:22–32 is that our marriages should reflect Christ and the Church. This is Paul's sole purpose for writing: that we would imitate and copy God in our conduct. Since we are new creatures in Christ (2 Cor 5:17) and we have died to our old ways, we are to walk in newness of life (Rom 6:4). This new life seeks to be like Christ in all our ways. When both husband and wife have this mindset, growth is inevitable. Solomon says in Proverbs 17:17, "Iron sharpens Iron, so one man sharpens another." If both parties seek to grow in Christ and seek to "encourage one another in love and good deeds," both parties will grow.
- Here are a few practical ways for you to grow spiritually in your marriage. (a) Study God's word together. One of the things my wife and I did both before we got married and after the wedding day is study our Bibles together. This was and still is very important to the success of our marriage. We have done this in different ways in the past. Sometimes we schedule a time when we read together and share our observations. Other times, we study the same passages privately and then come together to share our conclusions. Other times, we use curricula, study guides, workbooks, and other resources to help us study together and stay consistent throughout the year. Studying

together is vital to the success of your spiritual growth as a couple. (b) Pray with each other and over each other. From the moment my wife and I started dating to this present moment, we have prayed together before bed every night. This time allows us to share our hearts with each other and God. I learn what my wife is asking God to do in her life, and she learns what I am asking for in my life. Then we go to God with what we want Him to do in our marriage and family. This has blessed us in more ways than I can explain here. If you're not already, start praying together NOW! (Like right now, stop reading and start praying!)

- Lastly, find a community of believers that has the same goals as your spouse and you. Join a marriage ministry at your local congregation. Find mentors who can help you both grow to become the man and woman God would have each of you to be. These things help keep you encouraged and hold you accountable for walking in your divine callings as husband and wife. Titus 2 informs the older men and women to teach the younger, which means you NEED a mentor, someone to talk to, pray with, and receive wise counsel from (v. 2–8). Remember, nothing is new under the sun (Eccl 1:9)! That couple who has been married 50 years, trust me, they've been where you are, and God brought them through it. Ask them how He did it.

Conclusion

Marriage is not easy, but it is worth it! What a privilege we have that God gives us the opportunity to imitate Him in marriage. Remember, every instruction Paul gives in Ephesians 5:22–33 is based on what Christ has already done for us (the church). He does not call us to do anything He hasn't already done. So, rely on Christ to give you the strength to carry out His calling for you as husband and wife. Husbands love your wives as Christ loved the church (Eph 5:25). Wives honor and respect your husband as the Lord (Eph 5:22–23). If you do these things, growth is inevitable. Knowing what you know now, what will you do "from this day forward?"

Discussion Questions

1. In Ephesians 5:22–33, Paul implores the church to imitate God. Why does he do this? What is Paul's motive? How can we imitate God in our marriages?
2. Why does Paul not use the Greek word for "submit" in verse 22? What do you think is his reason for omitting the word? How should this shape our view of women in marriage?
3. Wives: How are you honoring and respecting your husband as the Lord?
4. Husbands: How are you loving your wives? How are you sanctifying, cleansing, washing, and presenting your wife blameless?
5. How does this text help us today? What practical things can you do to live this text out?

Endnotes

[i] All Scripture references are from the New American Standard Bible (NASB) unless otherwise specified.

[ii] A pericope is a distinct, self-contained passage or section of text, often from scripture, selected for reading or study. "Pericope," in *The SBL Handbook of Style*, 2nd ed. (Atlanta: SBL Press, 2014), s.v.

[iii] Francis Foulkes, *Ephesians: An Introduction and Commentary*, Vol. 10, Tyndale New Testament Commentaries (Downers Grove: InterVarsity Press, 1989), 159.

[iv] Walter Bauer, *A Greek-English Lexicon of the New Testament and Other Early Christian Literature*, 3rd ed., rev. and ed. Frederick W. Danker, trans. William F. Arndt, F. Wilbur Gingrich, and Frederick W. Danker (Chicago: University of Chicago Press, 2000), s.v. "ἀγάπη."

Chapter 3

Pillow Talk

How to Develop Effective Communication Skills According to Biblical Principles

Matthew Morine

Focus Passage

A word fitly spoken is like apples of gold in a setting of silver. Like a gold ring or an ornament of gold is a wise reprover to a listening ear. Like the cold of snow in the time of harvest is a faithful messenger to those who send him; he refreshes the soul of his masters. Like clouds and wind without rain is a man who boasts of a gift he does not give. With patience a ruler may be persuaded, and a soft tongue will break a bone (Prov 25:11–15).[i]

One Main Thing

Controlling the tongue in marriage is essential. A lot of people focus on what not to say. There is plenty mentioned on avoiding salty speech, but sometimes little about the sweet nature of speech. People think they are protecting themselves from making mistakes with words, but what is communicated is a lack of care. Using our words to build up one another is the correct use of the tongue. The better couples are those who can express feelings and ask for needs with a non-judgmental and gracious spirit. All humans want to be heard. When someone is heard, it allows them to feel loved and honored. In those times when there is conflict, how conflict is dealt with determines the overall quality of a relationship. This chapter aims to give you the communication skills to maintain a great connection in your marriage.

Introduction

Dr. John Gottman, a renowned psychologist who has extensively studied relationships and marriage, developed a method with remarkable accuracy for predicting whether a couple will divorce. He predicts this by analyzing short interactions in his research, often just a few minutes long. Here is what he looks for:

- Criticism: Attacking a partner's character rather than addressing specific behavior.
- Contempt: Displaying disrespect through sarcasm, mocking, or eye-rolling. Gottman considers this the most significant predictor of divorce.
- Defensiveness: Denying responsibility for problems or deflecting blame.
- Stonewalling: Withdrawing from conversation and emotionally shutting down.

All these behaviors are connected to the act of communication. If you make communication important in your marriage, you will improve the quality of your marriage.

In Proverbs 25:11–15, there are some quick principles that we can learn that will protect us from the communication patterns that destroy relationships. The behaviors noted in these verses can improve your marriage and life. One can learn about being non-defensive, using consistency, and being patient in speech. The more that you learn about these behaviors, the better you will nourish your spouse with love. Don't be like the old joke about the man who told his wife he loved her once, on their wedding day, and the punch line is that if he changed his mind, he would let her know. That's a terrible approach to communication and love. Instead, husbands ought to tell their wives they love them every day, perhaps even multiple times in the day. The same goes for wives to their husbands.

Going Deeper

Let's look at the first behavior for better communication. Can you be non-defensive in your listening? Proverbs 25:11–12 states, "A word fitly spoken is like apples of gold in a setting of silver. Like a gold ring or an ornament of gold is a wise reprover to a listening ear." The metaphor of jewelry dominates these two proverbs, and both concern the importance of good counsel. The "apples of gold" are not golden-colored fruits but are some kind of jewelry or artwork. Have you ever seen a lady wearing a piece of jewelry that is overkill on the finger or neck? It looks gaudy. The ring or necklace might be too big or too bright and almost overwhelm the person looking at it. Think about being blinded by too much bling. You can't look at it, and it makes the person look awkward. This is the point of the Proverb writer; he highlights that a good word is appropriate for the situation. Your emotional intensity, your choice of words, and your body language should fit with the message you are trying to deliver.

I remember one time listening to a sermon in chapel. The speaker was ultra-passionate about his message. His topic was the love of God. He was standing up front, screaming and yelling at the top of his lungs that God loved us. His face was red, and he seemed angrier about the point than he did about the truth of the statement. He looked mad. It was a total disconnect. He was too forceful in his delivery about a soft topic. He did not place his words in the setting of silver. Instead, it was like he was wearing a massive gold chain to a funeral.

Sadly, too often, people will cast off good insights because of the setting not being to their liking. Yes, the talker should think about the delivery, but the hearer needs to have a listening ear. The reprover should be wise, but too often, the hearer refuses to listen. There is an internal lawyer inside all human hearts. This lawyer seems never to lose a case. Anytime someone has something negative to say about them, the lawyer in their head goes ballistic on the defense. The offended hearer will look for every reason to reject the insights of the speaker. It could be the speaker was mean-spirited or that the hearer didn't realize the hidden intentions of the speaker, but regardless of the performance of the speaker, the hearer will reject the reprover. In marriage, can you hear your spouse? Can you take a breath and repeat back to them what the point is? A person's inner lawyer never wants to lose, but you must let your inner lawyer lose sometimes. The Proverb writer says clearly that one must have "a listening ear." The listening ear is better than one hung with gold. To be a good listener, repeat what the other person is saying to make sure you understand them.

The second skill in marriage that improves communication is to use consistency. Proverbs 25:13 says, "Like the cold of snow in the time of harvest is a faithful messenger to those who send him; he refreshes the soul of his masters." Both proverbs that follow v. 13 begin with some aspect of weather and its effects on an agrarian society; from that analogy, they move on to the importance of personal reliability. Verse 13 does not mean that it snows at harvest time —that would be an unmitigated disaster. It refers to bringing down snow from the mountains during the heat of harvest and the refreshment that gives to workers. If you have ever worked outside in the heat of a long, hot day, having a little cooling snow would be great. It likely won't happen, but it would be nice.

A happy marriage is one in which the spouses check in on each other. Every day, a couple should talk about the day's events and share their feelings about what happened that day. How did your spouse feel? A lot of times, the wife might have a wider bandwidth for emotions. In a single interaction, she can experience a range of emotions, from the heat of frustration to the warmth of compassion, while men tend to have a smaller spectrum for their emotions. She will tell him all about her day, all the ups and downs, every detail, but when it's her husband's turn, his day was merely, "fine." The next day, she gives a detailed account of the day, and he is "fine" again. To connect with another human, you need to share emotions with one another.

Being consistent in your communication allows the small fights to stay small. If you bottle up your emotions until you bubble over into anger, you will do a lot of damage to your marriage. Instead, cool your frustration like snow from the mountains would cool overheated harvesters. Use ten minutes each day to check in with one another. Husbands, make sure you share too. Try to give details.

The third piece of advice to have a happy marriage is to be patient in your speech. Proverbs 25:15 states, "With patience a ruler may be persuaded, and a soft tongue will break a bone." The bones are the most rigid body parts inside a person, and here, fracturing the bones refers to breaking down the deepest, most hardened resistance to an idea a person may possess. Using a soft approach can be less painful than an aggressive approach. You can forcefully break a bone, and it will hurt. However, if you use a gentle approach, the bone can be softened and snapped. People who get too engaged in attempting to persuade need to remember that it takes time for people to be able to think something through before they can truly change their minds. Gentleness and kindness can overcome the most powerful and obstinate.

One of the best principles to use for patience in speech is to set a time for a hard conversation. Too often, we are in the heat of a conflict, and words flow out like water through a broken dam. We allow all our passion to bubble to the top. Instead of being measured and controlled, we erupt. Set a time to talk if you know you need to talk through a hard topic. Both of you will be able to have the time to plan what you would like to say. You can enter the conversation with a calm level of emotionality, instead of speaking in a way that allows the conflict to escalate quickly.

Application

Here are three practical applications that you can put into practice quickly. All these suggestions can make a massive difference in your marriage.

1. The next time your spouse critiques you, try to listen calmly. Before responding, repeat what you think they are saying to ensure clarity and avoid misunderstandings. This helps to build trust and demonstrate your willingness to listen.
2. Set aside at least 10 minutes each day to talk with your spouse about how the day went. Encourage mutual sharing of not just facts, but emotions too. This daily habit can help you stay in tune with each other and address issues before they escalate.
3. The next time you're tempted to push your spouse to see things your way, pause and take a gentle approach. Speak softly, and allow time for your message to sink in. Avoid escalating the situation by rushing the conversation or becoming frustrated.

By embracing non-defensive listening, consistent communication, and patient persuasion, these principles can lead to more fruitful and harmonious interactions in marriage, helping both partners feel heard and understood.

Conclusion

Everyone wants to connect, but not everyone thinks about how to communicate. Connection follows good communication. The Proverbs writer understands the impact of our words. James, the brother of Jesus, does too, as he warns of the destructive nature of the tongue (Jas 3:5–12). However, we are only dealing with half of the issue by avoiding negative and harmful speech. We need to learn the skills of helpful speech. When each partner understands the other's perspective, it fosters empathy and strengthens the relationship. Good communication is essential in marriage because it serves as the foundation for understanding, trust, and emotional connection between partners.

Discussion Questions

1. What are the consequences of harmful communication patterns within a marriage? What are the early warning signs that will indicate an approaching storm of discontentment?

2. What negative information have you received about yourself that you initially rejected but, after some reflection, realized was true? What was your process to reach a better understanding of the critique?

3. Reflect on how much time you spend talking to your spouse. What time of day is best for you and your spouse to engage one another?

4. What are some signs in your own communication that you are being too forceful in your opinions and perspectives? How can you soften your words and still be clear and honest?

Endnotes

[i] All Scripture references are from the English Standard Version (ESV) unless otherwise specified.

Chapter 4

A Soft Answer

Words Of Wisdom For Conflict Management
Chris Miller

Focus Passage

A soft answer turns away wrath, but a harsh word stirs up anger (Prov 15:1).[i]

One Main Thing

Your home should be a place of strength and shared closeness among family members, enabling each member to overcome any challenge. The book of Proverbs is a rich resource of wise, to-the-point sayings of the great truths of this life, which can help equip us with tools to manage the troubles of such times. Sometimes, we need advice or short, precise instructions that will stick with us as we work to become better Christian spouses and parents. This is especially true about managing conflict when it arises in your relationship. Proverbs 15:1 should serve as a core trait for how Christians respond to others, including our spouses.

The verse states, "A soft answer turns away wrath, but a

harsh word stirs up anger." What would your home look like if this were your anthem for how you treat others? Our words matter—tone matters. Jesus said in Matthew 12:34–37,

> Out of the abundance of the heart the mouth speaks. The good person out of his good treasure brings forth good, and the evil person out of his evil treasure brings forth evil. I tell you, on the day of judgment people will give account for every careless word they speak, for by your words you will be justified, and by your words you will be condemned.

President Ronald Reagan once said, "Peace is not absence of conflict; it is the ability to handle conflict by peaceful means."[ii]

Introduction

Humility speaks volumes—and that isn't intended to be a cliché. Think about it. Humility does speak volumes about a person. Most of us in the church have, at some point, interacted with extremely humble people who left an impression on us where we couldn't help but think something like, "Wow, that is a humble person." Humility, ironically, can be quite impressive. It speaks volumes about a person's character.

Think about the last family conflict you experienced and how you responded to and worked through it. It may not be pleasant to think about, but it is healthy to analyze past behavior to recognize what you should have done differently and do better in the future. Spouses will, at times, disagree. We may have disagreements about financial decisions, raising children, how a child should be disciplined, tasks around the house, and many other areas that can lead to our not seeing eye to eye. The last time you had a disagreement with your spouse, were you motivated by humility, or did you mirror your spouse's aggression level and focus on trying to get your own needs met first?

We are surrounded by a worldly culture that has elevated anger to be what is perceived as really speaking volumes. Anger is to conflict what fuel is to fire. The more fuel, the stronger and hotter the blaze. As anger increases, so, typically, does the volume of the "conversation." The louder one gets, the more they feel they are dominating the conversation, and the more they feel like they are winning the argument. Great Christian homes function in a higher and better way, and that higher and better way is to broadcast humility in all interactions. Humility isn't a symbol of weakness or cowardice; humility is a sign of strength and self-control. Even amid conflict, the humble person values the other person and their feelings at least as much as his or her own (Phil 2:3).

A Deeper Look

Consider how many of the wise sayings of Proverbs point to a humble state of self-control and help us develop the mindset that enables us to communicate in ways that resolve conflict rather than feeding it. If we love these truths, they will significantly impact how we think and act. The following are just a few to consider as they provide context to Proverbs 15:1:

- When words are many, transgression is not

lacking, but whoever restrains his lips is prudent (Prov 10:19).

- There is one whose rash words are like sword thrusts, but the tongue of the wise brings healing (Prov 12:18).
- Whoever guards his mouth preserves his life; he who opens wide his lips comes to ruin (Prov 13:3).
- To make an apt answer is a joy to a man, and a word in season, how good it is! (Prov 15:23).
- The heart of the righteous ponders how to answer, but the mouth of the wicked pours out evil things (Prov 15:28).
- Whoever is slow to anger is better than the mighty, and he who rules his spirit than he who takes a city (Prov 16:32).
- The beginning of strife is like letting out water, so quit before the quarrel breaks out (Prov 17:14).
- Whoever restrains his words has knowledge, he who has a cool spirit is a man of understanding (Prov 17:27).
- If one gives an answer before he hears, it is his folly and shame (Prov 18:13).
- Whoever keeps his mouth and his tongue keeps himself out of trouble (Prov 21:23).
- A fool gives full vent to his spirit, but a wise man quietly holds it back (Prov 29:11).

Read the list again, this time more slowly, and contemplate each proverb to understand what it will look like to practice it. Think about who you are, how you think, and how you speak. Compare and contrast your communication habits to the proverbs and highlight differences. Think about how, by implementing these wise sayings into your thought process, they can shape your future communications so that you put out fires rather than fuel them. You can be a better husband, wife, child, or parent with biblical guidance. When you summarize these sayings, you understand that angry words, speaking too much, and simply unfiltered speaking of whatever is on your mind will often lead to problems, fights, arguments, and hurt. I've hurt others before by not thinking before speaking. I've hurt those closest to me by simply saying what was on my mind without thinking about it first. Speaking without thinking rarely works out for the good.

On the other hand, based on the above verses, speaking less, thinking before speaking, not giving fuel to anger, and remaining calm will, more often than not, lead to understanding and peace in your marriage. As part of your ongoing study, please read the book of Proverbs with a lens scanning for every verse that points to the importance of how we talk to each other. It will change your life (and marriage) for the better.

Above all, remember, "A soft answer turns away wrath, but a harsh word stirs up anger." Kindness and the control over one's emotions, necessary even when frustrated, are highly underrated. Kind communication is the most successful. Husbands and wives are supposed to be each other's "soft place to land" in this life. Even amid conflict, a soft answer is one way to make this your marriage's reality.

Application

- Prioritize active listening. The key to living out Proverbs 15:1 is learning to listen genuinely. We often feel compelled to speak our minds when we are driven by emotions or feel strongly about or against something. James 1:19–20 says, "Know this, my beloved brothers: let every person be quick to hear, slow to speak, slow to anger; for the anger of man does not produce the righteousness of God." To be a good listener, one must practice restraint when wanting to say something. The most common way people "listen" is by formulating their response or "fix" while the other person is still talking. That's not listening. The person who operates with the goal of responding with a soft answer, listens, intending to bring clarity and peace to what is going on. Good listeners often repeat what was stated to ensure clarity of understanding. Sometimes, it is good to let your partner know you are repeating their statement to make sure you heard them correctly. Do not repeat what they said sarcastically, but maintain the "soft" approach. The goal is "to turn away wrath." Stay calm and listen. Clarify understanding. Take your time and speak thoughtfully, kindly, and accurately. This works in marriage communication and every other kind.
- Avoid overgeneralizing. It is far too easy to reply in a disagreement with blanket statements like,

"You always ..." or "You never ...."
Overgeneralizing often fuels anger's fire
because "painting with too broad a brush"
triggers defensiveness. Overgeneralizing
statements are inaccurate. Stay calm and be
wiser by being more specific.

- Align your attitude with self-control. In
addition to passages from Proverbs, it would be
helpful to spend some time reading and
meditating on Galatians 5:13–22. If you have
time now, read through it. Keeping the right
attitude and not lashing out in anger is not just a
useful step toward resolving conflict but is also
tied to Judgment Day and our hope of eternal
life. The fleshly nature is the root of selfishness,
and uncontrolled anger comes from the will of
the flesh rather than the will of God. The flesh
brings forth things like hatred, contentions, and
outbursts of wrath. Verse 21 ends with, "Those
who practice such things will not inherit the
kingdom of God." Surrounding this section of
attitude correction is the foundation for why we
should be motivated to answer wrath softly. It is
love. Verses 14 and 22 both emphasize love. We
love our families. Unfortunately, we can
sometimes be guilty of speaking to and treating
family members worse than we may speak to or
treat anyone else. "These things ought not to be
so!" Since we love, we should strive to keep our
attitudes in check and maintain self-control.

Conclusion

The Proverb is true. A soft answer is the best and correct response, especially to wrath already kindled, and should be used to bring about peace. Our role as Christians isn't to mirror the fleshly attitude of someone else but to mirror the actions and attitude of our Savior. As Galatians 5:24 says, "And those who belong to Christ Jesus have crucified the flesh with its passions and desires." May it be so with us all!

Discussion Questions

1. Why does it seem easier to respond in anger to those we love the most than to those we are not close to?
2. What are some strategies from Proverbs we can train ourselves to practice to prevent letting anger take control?
3. What is the difference between uncontrolled and righteous anger? Can human anger ever achieve God's righteousness?
4. How do you understand the practical application of each proverb listed above?

Endnotes

[i] All Scripture references are from the English Standard Version (ESV) unless otherwise specified.

[ii] Ronald Reagan, "Address to the Nation on the Soviet Attack on a Korean Civilian Airliner" (speech, Washington, DC, September 5, 1983), Ronald Reagan Presidential

Library, https://www.reaganlibrary.gov/archives/speech/
address-nation-soviet-attack-korean-civilian-airliner.

Chapter 5

Forsaking All Others

Maintaining and Deepening Friendship in Marriage

Jon Hackett

FOCUS PASSAGE

> Enjoy life with the wife whom you love, all the days of your vain life that he has given you under the sun, because that is your portion in life and in your toil at which you toil under the sun (Eccl 9:9).[i]

One Main Thing

When entering marriage, it is so important that you and your spouse are "best friends," enjoying life together, cultivating shared interests, and keeping your romance alive. Friendship within marriage is one of God's most precious and greatest gifts to us. It is the foundation upon which a strong, lasting, and thriving relationship is built. Romance, physical intimacy, and shared responsibilities are vital, but friendship adds depth, joy, resilience, and a sense of adventure to a marriage. Ecclesiastes 4:9–10 reminds us,

> Two are better than one, because they have a good reward for their toil. For if they fall, one will lift up his fellow.

But woe to him who is alone when he falls and has not another to lift him up!

In this lesson, we will explore what it means to prioritize and nurture friendship in marriage. From shared experiences to working through challenges, the friendship between the husband and wife is always meant to glorify God and reflect His covenantal love. Grounded in biblical principles, this chapter will help guide spouses in building stronger bonds of friendship within their marriages, enjoying life together more, cultivating shared interests, and keeping the romance alive, even in the midst of life's challenges.

Introduction

When couples first meet and fall in love, friendship often comes naturally. For some couples, they start off as friends, and that friendship grows. Within those relationships, conversations flow easily, and shared interests emerge without much effort. Over time, however, the demands of life (work, children, financial responsibilities, etc.) can overshadow the friendship that initially brought two people together. Marriage, in such cases, can shift from being a joyful partnership to a transactional relationship focused only on survival. It takes true commitment and discipline from both spouses to maintain and keep the friendship fresh, exciting, and vibrant within the marriage.

God designed marriage to be more than a functional arrangement. In Genesis 2:18, He said, "It is not good that the man should be alone; I will make him a helper fit for him." This statement reveals the companionship God intended marriage to provide—a relationship where two people are not only partners in life but also best friends who deeply enjoy and support one another.

Being best friends in marriage means fostering physical intimacy, emotional intimacy, trust, and joy. It is about choosing your spouse as the person you confide in, laugh with, and lean on through all of life's seasons. Let's now explore five ways couples can cultivate, maintain, and deepen their friendship within their marriages by drawing on biblical principles and practical wisdom.

Going Deeper

First, marriage takes work! Two people don't just come together and have their marriage succeed without effort. You must have two disciplined people who are committed to making the marriage work. If the two aren't well-disciplined, then the marriage is going to have problems. That is why having a strong foundation of friendship is vitally important and helpful within the bonds of marriage. It is the commitment to each other that, no matter what, we will work to make our marriage last for life, which leads to success. Our mindset should be that divorce is not an option. Marriage is a commitment to each other that we will weather every storm of life together and work to make the relationship stronger with every one of its ups and downs.

Second, friendship is foundational in marriage. At its core, marriage is a covenant relationship. It is a commitment made before God to love, honor, and cherish one another. Within this covenant, friendship is a gift that sustains and enriches the relationship. Proverbs 17:17 teaches, "A friend loves at all times, and a brother is born for adversity." In marriage, this means being present for your spouse, not just in the joyful moments but also in the struggles.

Friendship in marriage encompasses physical intimacy, emotional intimacy, mutual respect, and sacrificial love. Sharing the physical bond with your spouse is extremely personal and important within the marriage. Physical (especially including sexual) intimacy is only meant to be shared between each other. The sexual bond helps build connection, trust, and emotional intimacy that not only strengthens the relationship but sets it apart from any other relationship or friendship you or your spouse have. True emotional intimacy is sharing your thoughts, feelings, and dreams with your spouse. This helps build a deep connection that surpasses the physical. With each other, husbands and wives should make themselves vulnerable and open in ways they shouldn't with anyone else. When we engage in emotional intimacy, we are showing the trust we have in our partner. This is why when a spouse has an affair with another person, physical or emotional, it is hard to repair the damage done to the marriage. The hurt caused by breaking that trust that the other has put into the relationship emotionally is hard to overcome.

You also must have mutual respect within marriage. Mutual respect is valuing your spouse's opinions, desires, and individuality. Notice the keyword is "mutual" respect. So many times, struggles happen in marriage because we don't value the other's opinions and desires over our own, or even equal to our own, or we fail to allow our spouse to have their own individuality. Having mutual respect means listening, acknowledging, and supporting your spouse's views, goals, desires, and input to the fullest extent biblically possible, especially when it comes to the marriage, the home, career, and the spiritual direction of the family. It is important to respect that your spouse is still an individual who has likes, habits, goals, dreams, etc. Encourage and support the individuality of your spouse. By showing mutual respect to one another, you are showing unselfish love and support. Putting your spouse's needs above your own is showing sacrificial love. This is also how we model what Christ has done for us (Phil 2:3–4). The example of Christ and His church serves as a powerful model for marriage. Ephesians 5:31–32 calls marriage a reflection of the profound mystery of Christ's love. Just as Christ calls His followers His friends (John 15:15), so too should spouses prioritize friendship as an essential aspect of their relationship.

Third, enjoy life together. Marriage is meant to be a source of joy. Ecclesiastes 9:9 encourages us to, "Enjoy life with the wife whom you love." Amid life's challenges, taking time to laugh, relax, and create memories together strengthens the marital bond. It is so important that you do everything you can to enjoy your life together. Work at it. Be creative. Get good advice. God wants you to be blessed with a marriage that brings you joy. Here are some important ways to enjoy life together. Make sure you laugh together. Proverbs 17:22 says, "A joyful heart is good medicine ...." Laughing together can relieve stress and foster closeness. Find the comical, funny, and absurd things in life to laugh about. Learn to laugh at yourself. So many times, we take our lives so seriously that we lose our ability to laugh at our flaws and mistakes. Make time to have fun, enjoy, and laugh together a priority. Another way is to celebrate the everyday. Take delight in small, simple moments— sharing a meal, watching a sunset, or reminiscing about happy memories. Finally, share in adventures together. Whether traveling to new places or trying new activities, shared adventures create lasting memories and bind us together with love. Do things that are outside your comfort zone: zip-line through the treetops, visit a town or city you've never been to before, whitewater raft down a river, etc. Couples who intentionally seek to have fun together can cultivate a friendship that weathers the storms of life.

Fourth, cultivate shared interests. Shared interests provide a foundation for connection and companionship. Amos 3:3 (NIV) asks, "Do two walk together unless they have agreed to do so?" Couples who find common ground through hobbies, activities, and ministry strengthen their bond and deepen their friendship. Finding hobbies you both love and can do together, like traveling, hiking, gardening, antiquing, playing a sport, etc., are great ways to strengthen your connection. Another way to cultivate shared interest is through finding ways to serve together or spend time learning together. Volunteer at church and in the community. Take a mission trip together. Participate in fundraising projects for a cause in need. You can also learn together by taking a class, doing a Bible study, or reading a book together as a couple. These activities not only bring joy but also create opportunities for meaningful conversation and teamwork.

Fifth, keep romance alive. Romance is a vital expression of love that keeps marriage fresh and exciting. Song of Solomon is a biblical celebration of romantic love, highlighting the importance of affection and desire within marriage. Song of Solomon 2:16 beautifully declares, "My beloved is mine, and I am his." In marriage, it is extremely important to keep the romance alive as you go through the seasons of life. Here are just a few of the ways to nurture romance. (1) Make it a goal to show daily affection. Small gestures of love like holding hands, giving compliments, writing notes, hugging, or bringing your spouse coffee go a long way in keeping the spark alive. (2) Be intentional about planning time together. Make it a priority to plan regular date nights and uninterrupted time to connect. This can become extremely hard to do when you have small children at home, but do it anyway. Call the grandparents or friends from church and get a babysitter, but make it a priority for your marriage. (3) Nurture your romance through thoughtful surprises. Have a favorite meal ready when your spouse gets home, or a handwritten letter. Plan a surprise weekend or night out at your spouse's favorite place. Send flowers to your spouse's work for no reason other than to say, "I love you." All these acts show that you value your spouse. Romance is not only about physical intimacy, but also about expressing how much you love and admire your spouse.

Application

Building and maintaining friendship in marriage requires intentional effort. Here are some practical steps to apply the principles discussed.

- Evaluate your friendship. Take time to reflect on the state of your friendship with your spouse. Are you spending quality time together? Do you feel emotionally connected? Identify areas for growth.
- Spend time together on a regular basis. Consistent quality time is essential for deepening friendship. Whether it's a weekly date night or a daily walk, prioritize these moments.
- Openly communicate with one another. Share your thoughts, fears, and dreams with your spouse. Use James 1:19 as a guide: "Let every

person be quick to hear, slow to speak, slow to anger."

- Work at resolving conflict in a positive way. Disagreements are inevitable, but how you handle them matters. Practice forgiveness and reconciliation, following Ephesians 4:32, "Be kind to one another, tenderhearted, forgiving one another, as God in Christ forgave you."
- Spend regular time in prayer together. Prayer strengthens spiritual intimacy and aligns each other's hearts with God's will. Commit to praying for and with your spouse daily.

Conclusion

Marriage is a wonderful and divine gift that God has blessed us with, and friendship is one of its greatest blessings. By becoming best friends with your spouse, you create a relationship that glorifies God and brings joy to your life. As Proverbs 18:24 reminds us, "There is a friend who sticks closer than a brother." Your spouse should be that friend! He or she should be the person who knows you deeply, loves you unconditionally, and walks with you through life's challenges and triumphs.

To maintain and deepen your friendship, focus on enjoying life together, cultivating shared interests, and keeping romance alive. Above all, center your marriage on Christ, whose perfect love is the ultimate example for all relationships. By doing so, you will build a marriage that not only endures but also thrives, bringing glory to God and joy to your hearts.

Discussion Questions

1. What qualities of friendship do you most value, and how can you cultivate those in your marriage?
2. How do you and your spouse currently enjoy life together? Are there new activities you can try to deepen your bond?
3. What shared interests could you develop or revisit to strengthen your friendship?
4. In what ways can you nurture romance in your marriage on a daily basis?
5. How does your relationship with Christ influence your friendship with your spouse?
6. What steps can you take this week to prioritize quality time with your spouse?

Endnotes

[i] All Scripture references are from the English Standard Version (ESV) unless otherwise specified.

Chapter 6

For Richer or For Poorer

Managing Money in a Way that Honors God

Jerrie W. Barber

Focus Passage

Do not lay up for yourselves treasures on earth, where
moth and rust destroy and where thieves break in and
steal, but lay up for yourselves treasures in heaven, where
neither moth nor rust destroys and where thieves do not
break in and steal. For where your treasure is, there your
heart will be also. The eye is the lamp of the body. So, if
your eye is healthy, your whole body will be full of light,
but if your eye is bad, your whole body will be full of
darkness. If then the light in you is darkness, how great is
the darkness! No one can serve two masters, for either he
will hate the one and love the other, or he will be devoted
to the one and despise the other. You cannot serve God
and money (Matt 6:19–24).[i]

One Main Thing

Either we will let the Lord guide us in controlling our money, or our money will control us. Wisdom begins with trusting the Lord to provide for our needs. He promises that provision when we place the Kingdom first in our lives (Matt 6:33). That commitment brings contentment (1 Tim 6:6–8). The love of money will allow all kinds of evil into our lives, lead us away from the Lord, and hurt us (1 Tim 6:9–10).

Introduction

Jesus gives the best investment advice. He said that to have our hearts right, we must prioritize our use of money with heavenly investments above earthly investments. I used to preach that when we get our hearts right, we will give right. Jesus said give right, and your heart will follow (Matt 6:21). Eyes focused bring light to our lives. We must decide who our master will be, either God or money. We prove which master we've chosen by the way we handle money.

Going Deeper

The best time to discuss money and its power in the family is before marriage. If you didn't do that, the next best time is now. In this home, will we place the Lord first? Before Gail and I married, we agreed on a percentage above 10% that would be our weekly contribution. Everything else had to fit in after that.

How much do we need to be content? Jesus and Paul said food and clothing (Matt 6:25, 1 Tim 6:8), but there is a wide range we can spend on these things. How much and what kind of food: prepared, homemade, restaurant, nutritious, or junk? In clothing, what and how much do we need to be content? How many shirts, slacks, shoes, and socks, and what brands? Do we continue buying when our closets are full?

After food and clothing, what will it take to make us content? In housing, will we finance the maximum for the longest time? Is it because of need or greed? Is it to provide a comfortable place to live or to impress our in-laws and friends? Is our car (or cars) for transportation or admiration? Will we overspend our budget and cut our church contribution to drive more than we can afford?

What plans do we have to be debt-free? Do we want to continue to be slaves to our creditors (Prov 22:7)? When do we plan to reach the goal of being debt-free? We each need to ask ourselves and answer honestly, "Are we on schedule now from when we set the goal a few years ago?"

How will we reduce conflict about how to spend the money we receive? What preparations are we making to deal with emergencies? Are we two paychecks away from foreclosure and bankruptcy? How long can we stay current with our obligations in the event of losing a job? How will we live when we can no longer work? Couples need to involve God prayerfully in patient, unselfish, loving, and respectful discussions aimed at settling the answers to these questions. Solomon tells us to imitate the ant by preparing in good times to provide for the slack times (Prov 6:6).

We need to pay attention to who or what is influencing our financial decisions. What are we reading, and who are our resources to give us Biblical and practical guidance as stewards of the resources the Lord has entrusted to us?

Application

Gail and I don't pretend that we are doing any better than anyone else. We're doing the best we know how to do at the present time. We live by the rules I encourage others to appreciate: Try not to learn very much. Aim to find a "mustard seed" in whatever you hear or read that can move a mountain in your financial life. What isn't helpful, throw in the proverbial wastebasket.

Discuss your regular giving as a family. Is your generosity communicating to God and yourselves that His Kingdom comes first in your lives?

Check your financial rules. You may think you don't have any. Rules are often unconscious, unspoken, understood, and contradictory. I have found it better to think about them, talk about them, and resolve the conflicts. I turned down the first raise I was offered by the elders where I was preaching. I was afraid people would think I was preaching for money. I didn't know what inflation was. The only thing I knew about inflation was that it was what I did when my tire pressure was low. I later learned that turning down a raise didn't reflect a good attitude towards money and providing for my family. Some kind and wise elders gently taught me.

Another rule that needed to be changed in my life was buying cars. When I was in my twenties, my advisors (friends) told me I needed to trade and get a new car every three years. They said inflation was so high that cars would get so expensive I wouldn't be able to afford one. That was my rule. Trade in my old car. But a new one. Finance it for thirty-six months (the maximum length of a car loan at that time). When the loan was up, repeat.

When I listened to better advisors, Gail and I together

decided to start paying cash for everything and set a goal to eliminate the mortgage on our house. It took a few years to reach those goals. When we committed to that, we started buying used cars. When we paid for the last financed car, we continued to make car payments. We made payments to a savings account. When we accumulated enough, we invested in a mutual fund with a good track record. We call it our "Car and Casket Fund." We have enough in it to replace Gail's car and my car. We have told our children that when one or both of us dies, there is enough money in the Car and Casket Fund to pay for our funeral. You can get a good funeral for the price of a car. If we are dead, we won't need the money in the fund for a car. Now, we trade cars when the price of a repair is half the value of the car, not when new cars smell so good we can't resist.

My experience is that contracts and agreements need to be written. A budget is a written contract about how our family will spend every dollar. If we want to spend more money in one area, we agree to reduce spending in another. Gail buys her clothes and personal items from "Gail's Clothes." I buy my clothes and personal items from "Jerrie's Clothes." We no longer fuss about who squeezes the toothpaste where.

Planning for emergencies reduces emergencies. We've saved for several decades. A new refrigerator or a heating and air-conditioning unit isn't an emergency at our house anymore. We know those items are not immortal. We have a "House Repair" item in our budget. When that comes up, the money is there. We have a small amount in the "Furniture" category in our budget. When we returned to our house to live while I fulfilled an interim ministry nearby, we had money to replace some items that were worn and ugly.

We "do our money" each week. We reconcile accounts

each month. As we do that, we discuss God, church, each other, children, grandchildren, great-grandchildren, and people in need that we might be able to help. All these things cost money. There is still some conflict and weariness when the checking account is $152.83 out of balance, but that is better than, "You need to quit spending so much money, you always get what you want, but I never get what I want." If we see a need to change an emphasis, we negotiate until we agree.

I was slow to accumulate an emergency fund and retirement account. I would save about $200.00, trade cars, wipe out my savings account to reduce my payment by a few dollars, and then start again. After a few cycles, I drew a line in the sand. If I don't keep my savings, I will never have any savings. One night, seventeen years before I was sixty-five, I evaluated where I was and where I wanted to be when I was sixty-five. I plotted where I wanted to be at retirement age and recorded where I needed to be at the end of each year until that date. I followed that plan and reached my goal.

I have read several good books on attitudes toward money and money management. I haven't remembered everything I have read. I have accumulated several "mustard seeds" that helped me to continue to improve. Many salespeople and financial advisors requested time to make presentations. I set the rules: "I am doing what I currently think is best. I will not reconstruct my financial plan after talking with you. I will probably learn something from you that will be helpful, and I probably won't buy anything from you. If you would still like to talk about understanding these agreements, when would be a good time for us to talk?" I learned much from these people. I talked for ten years with my friend who manages most of my retirement money before Gail and I gave him a dollar to invest. He gave much free advice before he made a dollar for his work.

Conclusion

Never forget that what matters most is how rich you are towards God (Luke 12:16–21). Read, think, and pray together about your priorities. Learn from as many sources as possible (Prov 11:14, 24:6). Check the sources your sources cite. Where did they get the information they are dispensing? How is their advice working for them? Gail and I asked our advisor how he manages his money in comparison to how he manages ours. Continue to learn by reading the Bible and other good books. Attend seminars online and in person. Listen to people who know more than you do and who practice what they teach. Thank God for the abundance He has given you in your prayers and with your purse. Share what you have with others. Teach your children and others how to be faithful to God with the material things He entrusts to us until we die or until He sends Jesus to take us to our final retirement.

Discussion Questions

1. I read about a writer who refused to write a biography unless he was given access to the person's checkbook. He said you don't know a person until you know how they handle money. What does your checkbook (financial records, income, and outgo) say about you and your family?

2. What are your financial goals? Are you on schedule to reach them?

3. Where and how do you get your financial advice?

4. Do you feel good about your progress in this stage of your life?

5. What improvements do you need to make? When do you plan to implement them?

6. How rich are you and your family toward God (Luke 12:16–21)?

Endnotes

[i] All Scripture references are from the English Standard Version (ESV) unless otherwise specified.

Chapter 7

To Have and to Hold

Understanding God's Design for Sexual Intimacy within Marriage

Joshua Pappas

Focus Passage

SONG OF SOLOMON 1:12–17[1]

Wife: The king is lying on his couch, enchanted by the fragrance of my perfume. My lover is like a sachet of myrrh lying between my breasts. He is like a bouquet of sweet henna blossoms from the vineyards of En-gedi.

Husband: How beautiful you are, my darling, how beautiful! Your eyes are like doves.

Wife: You are so handsome, my love, pleasing beyond words! The soft grass is our bed; fragrant cedar branches are the beams of our house, and pleasant smelling firs are the rafters.

One Main Thing

The result of the first wedding ceremony (Gen 2:24–25), which God performed when He brought Adam and Eve together for the first time, was that the two became "one flesh," a phrase that primarily refers to sexual intercourse (cf. 1 Cor 6:16). God bound Adam and Eve together as man and wife and then they consummated the marriage, being unashamed of their nakedness in their sinless innocence. Marriage makes it right in the sight of God for a man and a woman to enjoy the sexual pleasures of their bodies together. Even now, ages after the Fall into sin, when we all know it's shameful to expose one's nakedness to others,[2] a husband and wife, together alone, may still be naked together without shame. No other human relationship rightly allows this degree of intimacy. For this reason, couples look excitedly forward to their wedding night, and from that night onward, for as long as they remain physically capable, ought to be encouraged to explore each other's bodies and learn how to pleasure each other as much as possible, and to do so regularly. Sex within marriage is holy, good, right, pure, and hopefully fun, whether children proceed from the union or not.

Introduction

"The Talk." When we hear that phrase, we all know what "talk" it's referring to. One of the many things my wife and I worked out between us before we got married was that, if we were blessed with daughters, she would be responsible for having "The Talk" with them, and if we were blessed with sons, the lot would fall to me. We were blessed with two sons, so I did my duty. I'll tell you some funny stories about that another time. For now, let's have a talk together as Christian grown-ups—married couples, or those planning to be—or, three talks, to be precise. In Talk 1, we'll work through the connection between sex and procreation and come to some conclusions about shame. In Talk 2, we'll work through Bible passages that speak directly about sex in marriage. Finally, in Talk 3, we'll focus on freedom and biblical boundaries, in other words, what sexual acts are acceptable and unacceptable for bible-believers.

Going Deeper

Talk 1. The very first commandment in the Bible is for husbands and wives to have sex for the purpose of procreation (Gen 1:28). God further established the command in the Noahic Covenant (Gen 9:1), which is still relevant as long as this earth endures and there are still rainbows.[3] The earth being full of "the sons of disobedience" (Eph 2:2, 5:6) cannot be the fulfillment of these commands, as God desires that the earth be "full of the knowledge of the LORD as the waters cover the sea" (Isa 11:19). In Malachi 2:15, the prophet reveals (one of) God's aims for marriage: "Did he not make them one, with a portion of the Spirit in their union? And what was the one God seeking? Godly offspring." In Psalm 127:3–5, the Bible says,

> Behold, children are a heritage from the LORD, the fruit of the womb a reward. Like arrows in the hand of a warrior are the children of one's youth. Blessed is the man who fills his quiver with them!

Apparently, God considers it wise for Christian couples to have many children. So "be fruitful and multiply" still applies to God's people today by means of procreation, but also by adopting and raising children in the Lord who would otherwise be orphans, and bringing new converts into God's family through evangelism, but more will be said about this in the next chapter.

Does this mean every married couple must have children to be faithful to God? No. Does Scripture anywhere require a certain number of children? No. But we shouldn't deny that God generally intends His married children to procreate if they're able to, and the more the better if they'll raise them right (Prov 22:6). Marriage is privileged with God's approval to partner with Him in creating more unique, beautiful sons and daughters of God. Why would sacrificial love wish to deny any potential person the chance to exist and come to know God? Perhaps good stewardship has something to say here,[4] but the desire to have wealth and ease doesn't.

But procreation isn't the only purpose for sex, and sex is nothing to be ashamed of within marriage, even if it's just for the purpose of sharing the pleasure of it. On my maternal grandmother's wedding day, her mother told her in private, "Tonight he's going to want to do things with you and you're not going to like it, but you have to let him." That's humorous to us today (at least it is to me), and especially funny considering she went on to give birth to ten children, but it's also kind of sad. Sex within marriage is nothing to be ashamed of. If it were, God would never have invented it. Every married couple should read through Song of Solomon together multiple times in various versions. There isn't even a hint of shame between King Solomon and his Shulammite wife in that narrative, and never once does that great book about romantic love within marriage mention procreation as Solomon's and his beloved bride's main or only purpose. They desire each other. They relish the delights of each other's beauty. They are caught up in the joy of each other's love and in the pleasure of sexual touch. In marriage, sex is a gift from God, whether procreation is its aim or not, so if you're married, have fun.

Talk 2. Scripture has several important things to say about sex. First, it's only right within marriage and with the one you're married to. Numerous passages in both Testaments make this clear (Exod 20:14; Lev 18:20; Prov 6:32; Matt 5:27–28; 1 Cor 6:9–10, 18; Gal 5:19; Col 3:5; 1 Thess 4:3–5; Hebrews 13:4). Any sex outside of marriage is the sin of fornication, and if one of the participants is married to someone else, it's also adultery, which was a capital crime under the Law of Moses (Lev 20:10, Deut 22:22).[5] Christians are supposed to be so devoted to chastity that sexual sin is never once named among us (Eph 5:3). It's been too long since that word, "chastity," was celebrated among us regularly. Do we still know what it means?

> Chastity is the practice of abstaining from sexual activity outside of marriage and maintaining purity in thought and action, aligning with God's design for sexuality as outlined in Scripture (e.g., 1 Thess 4:3–5; Heb 13:4).[6]

Let's radically restore chastity among us, amen? We've got work to do here, but with God's help, we can restore what we've lost in this area over time. All it will take is the current generation of Christian parents to parent with prayerful determination while taking the separation from worldly influences part of holiness seriously (1 Cor 15:33). Imagine our influence among the lost if it were so well known that Christians practiced chastity that fornication was, for all practical purposes, never even named among us.

Scripture commands husbands and wives to have sex regularly. Consider the apostle Paul's teaching in 1 Corinthians 7:3–5,

The husband should give to his wife her conjugal rights, and likewise the wife to her husband. For the wife does not have authority over her own body, but the husband does. Likewise the husband does not have authority over his own body, but the wife does. Do not deprive one another, except perhaps by agreement for a limited time, that you may devote yourselves to prayer; but then come together again, so that Satan may not tempt you because of your lack of self-control.

Take note, husbands and wives, having become one flesh in marriage, you're no longer the owner of the rights to your body—your spouse is. You don't have the right to deny your spouse sex for any length of time or to use it as a tool for manipulation. Even if you don't enjoy it, it's not only about you. Bear your cross and meet your spouse's needs.

Talk 3. The Lord has said that to even look upon a woman to lust after her is sin. Pray for the will to think sexual thoughts of your spouse only. Adopt the Song of Solomon mindset as your ideal and celebrate your spouse as the gold standard of beauty (Song 6:9). Decide that no other woman or man can compare to your beloved. If you pray and ask the Lord to help you be attracted to your spouse, and your spouse only, don't you think He's going to help?

If you struggle with pornography, do whatever you must to rid your life of it,[7] and if you've never once looked, don't start, and you'll never have a problem. I've heard well-meaning folks say, "It's ok to look as long as you don't touch." That's not necessarily true. It all depends on how you look. It's okay to recognize and celebrate beauty to God's glory, but it's a sin to indulge in sexual thoughts about anyone other than your husband or wife. Remember 1

Corinthians 10:13—you don't have to fight temptation alone!

We need to trust that God has our best interests in mind. He doesn't want to hurt us, rob us, or deny us anything good (Jer 29:11). It's a lie of the devil to say otherwise. Having multiple sex partners hurts us deeply, whether we're able in the moment to realize it or not. There is no such thing as casual sex. Sex creates an emotional connection. This is why faithful Christians have the best sex. We stick to God's plan and develop deep, spiritual-emotional connections to our spouses, and it blesses us with safe, guilt-free, judgment-free, and deeply satisfying sex lives. If we communicate what we like and don't like, and always try to satisfy our spouse and not just please ourselves, we Christians really will have the best sex (Phil 2:4).

So, is it only the "missionary position" that's acceptable for Christians? Certainly not, and despite popular claims to the contrary, there is no evidence that Christian missionaries ever required anything of the sort of their converts over the course of church history. Within marriage, your liberty to explore what you like, however you like it, is limited only by the basic principles of righteousness. It's sinful if it involves anyone in addition to your spouse. Don't do anything that hurts either of you, physically, emotionally, or spiritually (Rom 13:10).[8] Beyond these restrictions, Christians are free to enjoy all kinds of sexual touch and all possible positions for intercourse. So, again, if you're married, have fun. You have God's approval.

Application

- Embrace sexual intimacy within marriage as a God-given gift that is holy, good, and pleasurable, whether for procreation or mutual enjoyment.
- Practice chastity by reserving sexual activity and thoughts exclusively for your spouse, avoiding fornication, adultery, and lustful thoughts about others.
- Fulfill conjugal responsibilities by regularly engaging in sexual intimacy, recognizing that each spouse's body belongs to the other, and avoiding deprivation except for mutually agreed-upon spiritual purposes.
- Enjoy freedom in sexual expression within marriage, limited only by the basic principles of righteousness, such as excluding third parties, and avoiding doing harm.
- Recognize procreation as a key purpose of marriage, but understand that sexual intimacy is also valid for pleasure and connection, even without procreation.
- Promote a culture of chastity within the church by teaching the next generation to abstain from sexual activity outside marriage and to view sex within marriage as a gift from God that is much more enjoyable if our consciences haven't been compromised by sexual sin. Urge separation from worldly influences to restore chastity as a celebrated virtue.

Conclusion

God's design for sexual intimacy within marriage, as beautifully depicted in the Song of Solomon, is a divine gift meant to bind husband and wife together in love, bless them with intense pleasure, and deepen the unity between them so that "one flesh" becomes more than just a physical reality, but also an emotional one. Far from being shameful, sex within marriage is holy, good, and divinely approved, whether it results in procreation or simply deepens the bond of companionship. By embracing chastity, fulfilling mutual conjugal responsibilities, and exploring intimacy within biblical boundaries, Christian couples can experience a fulfilling sex life that honors God. May every married couple, or those preparing for marriage, commit to celebrating this gift with joy, guarding it with purity, and teaching the next generation to uphold God's plan for sexuality, so that all Christian marriages may be a testimony of His truth, goodness, and beauty.

Discussion Questions

1. How can Christian couples cultivate a mindset that views sex as holy and pleasurable, and what practical steps can we take to overcome any feelings of shame or discomfort in this intimate relationship?

2. What are some challenges Christians face in maintaining chastity in today's culture, and how can the church and parents help restore this virtue in the next generation?

3. How can couples share open communication together about our sexual desires and needs to ensure mutual satisfaction, and what should we do if one spouse struggles to fulfill this responsibility?

4. How can we discern what is permissible and beneficial in our sexual relationships within marriage, and how can we ensure that our exploration strengthens our marriage rather than causing discomfort or harm?

Endnotes

[1] While this passage is taken from the New Living Translation (NLT) (with the headings changed) for the sake of clarity, all other Scripture references are from the English Standard Version (ESV) unless otherwise specified.

[2] There are circumstances in which practicality demands one's nakedness be seen by someone other than a parent of small children or a spouse without it being sinful, such as when certain medical examinations and procedures require it. Even in such cases, modesty must be secured to the fullest degree practically possible.

[3] Some claim too much when they teach "we no longer live by the Old Testament." We, indeed, no longer live under the Law of Moses (Gal 3–4, Heb 9–10), but not all the Old Testament is the Law of Moses. Genesis 1 and 9, for instance, though in the section of the Old Testament we call "Law," preceded Moses and remain in force. Genesis 9:16, part of the Noahic Covenant made between God and Creation after the flood, says, "When the bow is in the clouds, I will see it and remember the everlasting covenant between God and every living creature of all flesh that is on

the earth." The command to be fruitful and multiply starts the text of that covenant. When Paul wrote 2 Timothy 3:16–17 he had the Old Testament in mind, though the truth applies equally to the New Testament (2 Pet 3:15–16). Even though we no longer live under the Law of Moses, it teaches us in principle, as the New Testament consistently reveals in its references to and quotes from the Law.

[4] In other words, it isn't wise to procreate your family into dependence or needless poverty.

[5] Stated here to stress just how abhorrent a sin it is in God's eyes.

[6] Grok 3, "Definition of Chastity," xAI, accessed May 22, 2025, https://x.ai/grok.

[7] See Matthew 5:29–30 and understand Jesus was using hyperbole. If you will do whatever it takes to rid your life of a besetting sin, God will strengthen you against it long before you start cutting off body parts.

[8] In the ESV, Romans 13:10 says, "Love does no wrong to a neighbor; therefore love is the fulfilling of the law." The Greek word translated as "wrong" is "*kakos*," which includes the idea of "harm," which is the rendering in the New International Version (NIV).

Chapter 8

Be Fruitful and Multiply

Having and Raising Children in a Christian Home

Evan Kirby

Focus Passage

> And God blessed them. And God said to them, "Be fruitful and multiply and fill the earth and subdue it, and have dominion over the fish of the sea and over the birds of the heavens and over every living thing that moves on the earth" (Gen 1:28).[1]

One Main Thing

God calls humans to be fruitful and multiply and spread His dominion over all the earth through being His image bearers (Gen 1:26–28). Ultimately, families—fathers, mothers, sons, and daughters—are intended to propagate the Kingdom of Heaven on earth by becoming sons and daughters of God and making other sons and daughters of God through intentional discipleship.

Introduction

God loves families. He created the first family—Adam and Eve—and told them their purpose was to be His imagers[2] (Gen 1:26–27), to be fruitful and multiply to make more imagers, and for those imagers to spread His dominion over all the earth (Gen 1:28). God wants families to be part of His family. Is this command given to Adam and Eve intended to be for all time, in all places, and for all people?

God wants His creation to leave, cleave, and multiply. That much is clear from the first few chapters of the Bible. It was part of His original design for humankind. Husbands and wives are a blessing to one another, and the love they experience is to be highly regarded (Mal 2:15, Eph 5:25–31). Children are a blessing for a family and are also to be highly regarded (Ps 127:3–5). And yet the Bible is filled with examples of couples who could not have children, and God had to miraculously open their wombs as a display of His mighty power (Gen 17:15–21, 25:21; 1 Sam 1:11; Luke 1:7–17). And the world to this day is filled with women who cannot have children for various reasons. Are we to assume that these people are in rebellion against the first command of God?

I think this would be a silly application of this scripture, for Jesus Himself—the perfect Son of God and exact imprint of God's image—was neither married in the human sense nor had any physical children. But rest assured, Jesus was and is responsible for all of God's sons and daughters (John 1:12–13). Additionally, the great Apostle Paul, in his intense desire for the return of Christ, told the Corinthians that he would rather they be single and childless like him so they could focus more closely on the work of the church (1 Cor 7:7–8). But rest assured, Paul did not hesitate to call

Timothy his "true child in the faith" as he had discipled him and taught him to follow in his footsteps (1 Tim 1:2).

Nevertheless, it is the case that in most circumstances discipling your own family is the easiest way to multiply God's image in the earth. The world has been telling us for decades that it is wrong to have children and add more people to this earth. Muslims and Mormons have largely been able to ignore this lie from the world and have, therefore, been populating the earth with more and more Muslim and Mormon children. For some reason, many Christians have bought into the worldly idea that we should stop having children, stop making families, and stop having such high regard for the traditional nuclear family. But let us remember that if we have been raised with Christ, we are called to seek the things that are above, not the things that are on the earth (Col 3:1–2). A deep dive into the command "Be fruitful and multiply" will be helpful in seeing the purpose behind God's original mandate.

Going Deeper

On the surface, the mandate to "be fruitful and multiply" sounds like it is simply for the sake of populating an empty earth. Indeed, God also commanded the birds and the fish to be fruitful and multiply (Gen 1:22), and after He flooded the world—bringing its human population down to just eight souls—He again commanded that Noah's family "be fruitful and multiply" (Gen 9:7). In the beginning God needed the earth to be populated and that seems to be this command's purpose, but this phrase as it continues to be used in scripture becomes more focused.

The LORD promised the Israelites at Mt. Sinai that if they obeyed His voice, He would make them fruitful and multiply them to fulfill His covenant with them (Lev 26:9). These are the people He promised to bless so that they could in turn bless "all the families of the earth" (Gen 12:1–3). The prophet Jeremiah speaks of the continuation of this promise—despite disobedience from God's people—when he prophesies that the days are coming when LORD will gather His scattered children from captivity so they can "be fruitful and multiply" (Jer 23:3). This will be accomplished —Jeremiah prophecies—by God's raising up of the Righteous Branch of David who will become the LORD's righteousness for His rebellious people (Jer 23:5–6). Those days were fulfilled "in the fullness of time" in which Jesus came to redeem us and make us sons and daughters of God (Gal 4:4–7).

Simply put, God wants the whole earth to be under His dominion. This means that human families need to become God's family. God wants all His creation to once again become "partakers of the Divine nature" and reflect His image into all the world for His glory (2 Pet 1:4). This was done through Abraham's family in the person of Jesus Christ, who now makes any who come to Him in faith, being immersed in Him, part of Abraham's family and therefore God's family (Gal 3:23–29). As Jesus puts it in the "Our Father" prayer, "Your Kingdom come, your will be done on earth, as it is in heaven," God's desire is for His whole creation to look like Him, think like Him, and do His will (Matt 6:10).

This is accomplished by families being discipled for Jesus. Men leave their father and mother, cleave to a wife, multiply their family by having children (if possible), and then ensure that the whole family is discipled into the family of God, to then repeat the process. This Biblical process of being fruitful and multiplying God's image on the earth does not exclude us from the responsibility of evangelizing and bringing other families into the fold of God, but discipling our own families toward Jesus should be a priority, as it has the highest chance of success in multiplying God's image. While it is not within the purview of this study to teach you how to make children (thankfully), some practical thoughts on how to disciple our families for Jesus are in order.

Application

The struggle with discipleship is that we are constantly being discipled by God's enemy through the desires of the world (1 John 2:15–17). Satan is disciplining us for death, and God wants to discipline us for life (Eph 2:1–7, Jas 1:13–15). The books we read, the media we consume, the friends we listen to, the schooling we learn from, all the voices of worldly wisdom and formation of worldly habits are Satan's way of discipling us to his cause (Jas 3:13–18). If we are to be families who are faithfully discipled for Jesus, it will take focus and effort to eschew Satan's discipleship in favor of Jesus's easy yoke (Mat 11:28–30).

The Israelites, under the law of Moses, constantly had their minds brought back to the LORD God and His statutes through careful observance of a robust spiritual calendar. Each day included recitation of the *Shema*, "Hear, O Israel: The LORD our God, the LORD is one. You shall love the LORD your God with all your heart and with all your soul and with all your might" (Deut 6:4–5). Moses followed up this command with the guideline that these things ought to be taught to the children throughout the day lest they "forget the LORD" (Deut 6:6–15). There was also a weekly reminder of the LORD in the practice of Sabbath

(Deut 5:12–15), a monthly reminder in the burnt offerings at the new moon (Num 29:6), and the seven yearly feasts as celebrations to the LORD (Lev 23:1–44).

These observances are obviously not commanded of Christians today who are under Christ's New Covenant (Gal 4:8–11). The only regular observance commanded of us is weekly gathering with God's people for encouragement, worship, and participation in the Lord's Supper (Heb 10:24–25; Acts 20:1–7). But they serve as an example that faithfulness toward God takes regular reminders to bring our focus and attention back to where it needs to be.[3]

You may have noticed that discipline and disciple have the same root. We do not become faithful disciples of Jesus without regular discipline toward that end. Paul entreated Timothy, his "son in the faith," to "train" or discipline himself "for godliness" because "it holds promise for the present life and also for the life to come" (1 Tim 4:7–8). He compares this training to physical exercise, which is profitable for this life only. In making this comparison, Paul implies an important teaching. Training your body for physical health is a slow process that requires consistent hard work. Discipling our families toward the image of God is no different. Like the Israelites under the Law of Moses, noted above, there needs to be regular training of our minds, wills, emotions, and consciences to be set on God.

Families should be purposeful in organizing their time around praying to God, hearing from God in His word, worshipping God, speaking of God, and creating habits out of making Godly decisions. Could you cut out an hour of TV—that is likely being used as a tool for Satan to drive a wedge between you and God anyway—and spend that time setting your mind on God instead? Could husbands and wives be seen being affectionate and loving toward each other so that they can tell their children that this is what God truly wants for husbands and wives? What if we were able to take every mistake our children make and turn it into a lesson about who God is, why He loves us, and how He sheds His mercy on us every day? What impact could you have if you and your children prayed together in the car on the way to school in the morning, reminding them who they are and to Whom they belong?

Conclusion

Your family is important to God because God wants you to be part of His family. He freely and mercifully adopts any into His holy family who come to Him calling on His name through faith, repentance, and baptism (Matt 11:28–30; Acts 2:21, 37–39; Rom 10:8–13). His call for you to be fruitful and multiply is a call for you to bring your family into citizenship in His kingdom and live as imagers of God, reflecting His image into all the world for His glory. Families that want to fulfill this call will need to wake up each day and maintain the mindset that they are living sacrifices for Jesus and that remaining faithful to that cause requires that they be transformed to Christ's image, not conformed to the world's (Rom 12:1–2). May God lead you by His Spirit to help your family reclaim their place as partakers of the Divine Nature!

Discussion Questions

1. What practices do you have for discipling your family toward the LORD God?

2. What are some specific ways you have noticed Satan trying to disciple you and your family?

3. Aside from attending church, how is your daily schedule or weekly calendar specifically planned with being a disciple of Jesus in mind?

Endnotes

[1] All Scripture references are from the English Standard Version (ESV) unless otherwise specified.

[2] Imagers, or image-bearers—made in God's image and called to reflect His holy nature back towards Him in reverential, obedient love.

[3] For more information on creating a rule or rhythm of life centered around Christ for your family, visit https://sacredordinarydays.com/pages/rule-of-life. If you would like to see the Kirby Family Rule of Life as an example, feel free to email me at erkirby15@gmail.com.

Chapter 9

In-Laws or Outlaws

Navigating Relationships with Extended Family

Jacob Rutledge

> And the rib that the LORD God had taken from the man he made into a woman and brought her to the man. Then the man said, "This at last is bone of my bones and flesh of my flesh; she shall be called Woman, because she was taken out of Man." Therefore a man shall leave his father and his mother and hold fast to his wife, and they shall become one flesh. And the man and his wife were both naked and were not ashamed (Gen 2:22–25).[i]

One Main Thing

Family life is a wonderful blessing from our Lord, and yet it is not without its struggles. Marriage, the cornerstone of a new family, is the unification of two distinct groups: the family of the groom and the family of the bride. Too often, this important dynamic is overlooked, which can foster anxiety, bitterness, and resentment. A failure to engage in the complex relationship with in-laws diminishes our ability to experience the richness of life, which God promises. Honing our abilities to successfully engage with our in-laws will cultivate a healthier and more spiritually mature family unit.

Introduction

The first time I met my father-in-law was many years before I married his daughter. As a child, I was taken to a seminar being held in a town nearby to where we lived. At this event, the speaker focused on events in Genesis, discussing subjects like dinosaurs and God's creative power. I was transfixed. To this day, I remember being fascinated by the pictures of these incredible monsters being posted as slides on an old projection screen. I never imagined that many years from then, I would one day meet and marry the oldest daughter of the preacher to whom I was listening.

Divine Providence has a funny way of redirecting our paths and fostering connections with new people whom we may not have otherwise chosen on our own. Relationships come and go, and you never know which ones will last and impact you in the long term. Eventually, if you decide to marry, your concept of family will involve people with different traditions, habits, values, and quirks with which you aren't familiar. Learning to engage with the new family dynamic of your in-laws is an often-overlooked skill that, if neglected, can lead to unnecessary stressors in your marriage and family. In addition, when we refuse (or are unable) to engage in a spiritually mature relationship with our in-laws, we are robbing ourselves of one of the great blessings of family: the variety and diversity of human personalities within the family unit.

Going Deeper

When we look at the founding of the family in Genesis 2:22–25 there is an expected new attachment in which the husband is called to "leave" his father and mother and "cleave" or "hold fast" to his new wife (v. 24). In this separation and unification, there is the creation of a new family unit in which the spouses become "one flesh." This intimacy does not imply a negation of the individuality or experiences of each spouse, far from it. Rather, it is a mysterious image by which individuality gives way to harmony and an act of total, self-giving love. This is the beautiful foundation —love, sacrifice, and intimacy—upon which God builds our most cherished institution: family. It shouldn't surprise us that when the family unit deteriorates, the void created produces the opposite of love, sacrifice, and intimacy: hate/bitterness, selfishness, and isolation.

In this intimacy founded within marriage, we witness what God hopes for, not only within the immediate family but within the extended family as well. Yes, the husband is called to leave his parents, but many other passages prove this does not mean abandonment, and the wife is not even explicitly called to this in Genesis 2 (though one can infer it is expected of her as well). Matthew 15:1–6 teaches us that the husband still has the responsibility to take care of and honor his aged parents despite being married, so, though marriage creates a new, distinct family unit to which husband and wife must give priority, it doesn't entirely sever husband or wife from prior family connections. It rather builds upon what existed previously as an addition to and outgrowth of the extended family, expanding and strengthening the community rather than shrinking and weakening it. Using a metaphor of a garden (since our main text is in

Eden, it seems appropriate), one might see, rather than a "repotting," a new shoot growing up from a tree's roots or new seeds germinating in a shared garden bed. This is the expectation of God for human existence—not isolated groups of random individuals, but a progressively maturing and developing community sharing in the blessedness of life.

It is difficult in our current individualistic society to conceive of a community in which the personal autonomy of the couple is recognized, but there are still expectations of responsibility toward the extended family. It is important to remember the historical and cultural context in which we find ourselves, recognizing how deeply impacted we are by the society around us. Increasingly, it seems that our culture is growing more and more privatized; parents are alienated from their children as couples are taught to cut off anyone who is "toxic" in their lives. No doubt, there are dangerous family dynamics that must not be tolerated, but at the same time, this type of selfish and indulgent mentality is not of God. We are not islands, cut off from the mainland and constantly needing to defend our territory (though boundaries might need to be placed at times). Rather, as Paul says about the Lord (but just as applicable to family): "For none of us lives to himself, and none of us dies to himself" (Rom 14:7).

Thus, in-laws are intended to be an extension of the shared intimacy of the marital union; they are meant not only to protect and cultivate the new marriage but also to share in the hoped-for fruit of its union: grandchildren. So, the parents of the spouses do have a certain claim on the children of this new marriage (though the parents, having the higher responsibility for raising them, Ephesians 6:4, maintain a higher claim). Grandchildren are a blessing from the Lord given to the elderly (Prov 17:6). When making claims like this, some might respond negatively: all they can imagine are the nightmare scenarios of overbearing grandparents who attempt to shoulder their way into the family dynamic (which, too often, is a very real scenario married couples face). Yet, if we can imagine for a moment what Eden would have looked like if Adam and Eve hadn't sinned, we can fathom what the ideal family dynamic would be: Cain and Abel raising their little ones under the shade of those ancient trees, as Grandpa Adam and Grandma Eve look on in loving support of the blessings which God has granted.

The Lord loves life, and thus, in the beginning, He called it "very good" (Gen 1:31). At the summit of His creative work was the family, a unit in which He implanted the possibility of new members that would create and combine into a flourishing community of life and blessing. This necessitates in-laws, which are intended to be a part of the new growth. Of course, whenever there is new growth, there are times of struggle in which different perspectives, values, and habits require compromise, patience, and fortitude. Yet, if we can learn to develop healthy patterns of a godly family dynamic, we can produce a family that will continue to be a blessing for generations to come.

Application

- In considering the impact that our in-laws have on our family dynamic and life in general, it is essential that we encourage our children to examine not only their potential spouse but the values and habits of their family. Encouraging

Christians to marry Christians is important, but too often we overlook other important characteristics simply because they are believers. No doubt, how the family functions will impact the marriage for years to come (1 Cor 15:33). It is important for us to teach our children to look at how future in-laws engage in conflict and handle anxiety, their priorities in relationship compared to other commitments (work, church, sports, hobbies, etc.), as well as how they handle their finances. While it is difficult to learn all these things before marrying, it is still possible to grasp the overall way a potential spouse's family handles various obligations.

- Setting boundaries is an important and necessary habit for a new couple to develop early in their marriage. Some in-laws have a difficult time respecting the new life of their child and his or her new spouse and may attempt to overshadow and influence their decisions out of fear. Unfortunately, some in-laws can be manipulative, playing on the affections of their children to maneuver their child toward their desires (sometimes coming into conflict with their child's spouse). Thus, it's important to understand how to set boundaries without cutting in-laws off completely. Being honest and upfront is an important value for a Christian (Eph 4:15), and not allowing the potential emotional distress of in-laws to impact a couple's decision-making process is essential. This is especially important for the husband, as

he, at times, will need to take the lead in conflict
resolution as the protector of his new marriage.
It is possible to have relationships with our in-
laws that both foster stable relationships and
respect healthy boundaries.

Conclusion

Relationships with in-laws are the butt of many a joke and
the plot line for a host of movies. Each of them seems to
recognize the overall difficulty of creating new, intimate
relationships with people who hold different values and
habits. Hopefully, we can see that, though God certainly
wants each marriage to become an individual unit that
creates a new chapter in the human community, he doesn't
expect them to do this alone. This world is filled with so
many enemies to the family, all waiting to do what they can
to tear it down and rend it asunder. Thus, a new family
needs the help of those with more experience and wisdom,
not meddling, and the security that only true, properly
prioritized love can provide. First things first—the marriage
must come first, before the desires of the in-laws, but not
antagonistic to them.

God intended for a new marriage, like a fledgling chick,
to have the protective wings of extended family to lovingly
support and aid it as it comes into its own new life. Yes, this
can unfortunately lead to conflicts as spouses and in-laws
figure out where the boundaries are in this new relationship.
At the same time, what a blessing in-laws can be when they
understand their role as life-giving and supportive rather
than restrictive and overbearing. If we, by the grace of God,
can learn to work patiently within this framework that the

Lord offers us, then the goodness of God's design will shine forth in our communities.

Discussion Questions

1. In the text of Genesis 2:22–25, we see that the "leaving" seems to fall exclusively on the part of the man, whereas little is said about the woman's responsibility. Is this intentional? Was it cultural? Are there ways in which gender dynamics might impact how we engage with the family unit of the wife rather than the husband? If so, why? If not, why not?

2. What are some helpful questions we might ask as we examine the family dynamics of our future spouse? How might we counsel our children to inspect, without intruding, the various habits of their future in-laws?

3. There is a host of scriptures that aid us in producing healthy, relational dynamics within the home. What are some that you might memorize to aid you in a time of need when dealing with your in-laws?

Endnotes

[i] All Scripture references are from the English Standard Version (ESV) unless otherwise specified.

Chapter 10

Branching Out
Serving Christ Together
Matthew Thigpen

Focus Passage

> The churches of Asia send you greetings. Aquila and Prisca, together with the church in their house, send you hearty greetings in the Lord (1 Cor 16:19).[1]

One Main Thing

Have you ever considered the "solo" ladies attending your congregation and their activities? Those ladies are some of the most active ladies in most congregations. However, they can sometimes also be the most disheartened ones. When I say the "solo" ladies, I'm not primarily talking about the widows or single ladies, but those whose husbands either don't attend with them or only attend worship and nothing else. While typically fewer in number, there are also sometimes active men whose wives aren't committed to the cause. I have always been amazed at how much these "soloists" can achieve, but it pales in comparison to what can be achieved by a couple working together to serve the kingdom. In this lesson, I want to challenge us as married couples to consider striving to avoid making either partner the soloist, instead to branch out and serve our Lord and local congregation by working in unison to further His kingdom.

Introduction

To understand the need for a complementary relationship between a husband and wife, we can go back to the very beginning and look at God's plan for the family. In Genesis 1 and 2, we read about the creation of the Earth. Each day, God looked over what He had made, and nearly every day, said that the day's creation was good (Gen 1:4, 10, 12, 18, 21, 25, 31). However, amid His creation process, we get a zoomed-in look at the creation of man and woman in Genesis 2, in which God acknowledged that something was not good (Gen 2:18). He noted that it was not good for the man to be alone, so God created woman for him from his own flesh and bone. This occurred after all the animals had been brought to Adam, and no suitable helper was found for him. I believe God emphasized doing it this way to show Adam that something was lacking. Something was needed that no other creature could provide. Only through another created being like him could Adam have the helper he needed.

A key point of interest is that the man needed a helper in his life, a companion like him, but not the same as him. The Hebrew word for "helper" here is typically used throughout the Old Testament in reference to calling on God for help or as a reference to God being a person's helper in time of need. This kind of helper is one who can save and deliver (Ps 121:1–2, 115:9–11). God can do so without limits. A spouse can do so within limitations, but the help can be significant. In some passages, the word for "helper" may even carry strong military overtones (cf. Deut 33:7, 26, 29).[2] The need for a helper does not mean that the helped or helper is weak, but that they, alone, are inadequate to accomplish life's mission.[3] So, in Genesis 2:18 and 20, God reveals that humans are insufficient alone, and thus, He creates a helper to assist day by day and help win the battles of life.

The more I ponder the need for a complementary husband and wife team working together for Christ, the more I cannot help but wander in my mind back to arguably the greatest example of a Christian couple working together in the whole Bible, Aquila and Priscilla. I find it interesting that of all the New Testament disciples we read about, none are always found as a pair or mentioned together as much as Aquila and Priscilla are. They serve as an example of the value of husband and wife working together to further the church. Let us examine passages that speak of Aquila and Priscilla and see what we can learn.

Going Deeper

The first time we read of Aquila and Priscilla in Acts 17:1–4, we see they are helping those around them. As they were fellow tradesmen (tentmakers), they took Paul in, helping provide him work and a place to stay when he came to Corinth. Their help was a great assist to Paul as Acts 16 reveals that Paul ran into trouble at Berea and had to leave Timothy and Silas, his traveling partners, behind, and go alone to Athens, and later Corinth. Afterwards, this great Christian couple went with Paul on the next leg of his missionary journey, where they stayed behind to work in Ephesus as Paul continued onward (Acts 17:18). It is at Ephesus that they performed their most memorable work.

While in Ephesus, the couple encountered a teacher named Apollos (Acts 17:24–28). Apollos, a Jew who had been instructed in the way of the Lord, only knew of the baptism of John. He had not yet been taught Jesus's baptism (i.e., Christian baptism), which had fulfilled and replaced John's preparatory baptism. When Aquila and Priscilla heard him preaching, they noted his error and sought to correct him. It is of interest to note the way they corrected him. They waited until he had finished speaking and then took him aside privately and corrected him. They taught him the way of God more accurately, and after he accepted their teaching, he carried on preaching the whole gospel truth everywhere he went. Apollos then became a name synonymous with great teachers in the church. Paul mentioned him in the book of 1 Corinthians as a well-known teacher when discussing that church's issue with divisively following teachers rather than following Christ in Christian unity. It should make us think and wonder, what would've happened if Aquila and Priscilla had not taken the time to correct Apollos? What would have happened if only Aquila had corrected Apollos alone? However, we don't have to let those thoughts run too far because we are told of the great blessings this couple bestowed upon Paul and Apollos in their times of need.

It is also fitting that Aquila and Priscilla are mentioned in the closing chapter of Paul's epistles to the Romans and 1 Corinthians. In Romans 16:3–4, we learn that Aquila and Priscilla were responsible for saving Paul's life at some point. Some think this may have been their taking him in at Corinth, but we are unsure what event Paul is referencing.

However, it appears to be a well-known event to the first-century church. Then in 1 Corinthians 16:19, we learn that Aquila and Priscilla were hosting a church that met in their home. Some speculate that this could have been in Rome, where the epistle of Romans may have been delivered, since Aquila and Priscilla were originally from Rome, but had to flee to Corinth during the reign of Claudius, when he commanded all Jews to leave Rome (Acts 17:2). From all that we see this great couple accomplishing, it is only fitting that we find them hosting a church in their home. Finally, we see them mentioned one last time in Paul's last epistle. In 2 Timothy 4:19, while facing his imminent death, Paul expressed concern about the Christians who had worked with him and assisted him throughout his entire ministry, and mentioned this great first-century Christian power couple by name.

Application

With the excellent example of Aquila and Priscilla in mind, we can start to appreciate the importance of a husband and wife to recognize their need for each other and that they should aim to help fill in the gaps where each other has complementary strengths and weaknesses. Regarding our Christian faithfulness and service to God, we should recognize the importance of a couple working together to share God's word and love. Let's look at a few ways this complementary relationship can help us in our shared mission of serving the church.

- As a minister for the past twenty-plus years, with the last thirteen being married, I have realized the importance of having a supportive spouse. In my ministry, there are things that I do not like to do. In the last thirteen years, I have learned the great blessing of having a complementary helper. One example is that I am not the best at visiting people. However, this is an area where my wife is stronger than I am. So, we have worked out a strategy where when we make ministerial visits, we typically try to go as a couple, and now that we have kids, it is a family affair. This has helped our relationship tremendously because we get to serve other people as a couple by spending time with them. We also get to teach our children the importance of sitting and talking to others, listening, and learning from their lives. We have also grown closer as a couple because we spend more time together serving others and our Lord. It also helps to have another person listen to a person talk because we typically hear and pick up on different cues. There have been many visits where one of us will ask the other, "Did you catch when they said ...?" This is typically a cue to a need or worry that the person has that we would have been unaware of otherwise. Remember, ministerial visitation isn't "preacher's work," it's Christian work!

- Another way a couple works together beneficial to the church is by talking to people about Christ and helping those who are struggling. When I talk to most people, as a man, I tend to be more focused on the factual and logical side of the discussion, whereas my wife thinks more on the emotional side of things and can make connections to people and help them in a way that I am not able to do alone. There have been some situations where I have been unable to help someone, but she has been able to step right in and connect in a way I failed to do. There have been many examples in our church work where we have had someone, typically a female, come wanting to study or ask a question, and I have explained the need for baptism or attempted to answer their question, only to leave the person feeling lost after talking to me. Then my wife spoke to them afterwards and was able to connect the dots for them in a way that I had failed to do.

- Different personality types can be a barrier to successful ministry. Husbands and wives working as a team bring two of them to the table, and two is better than one (Eccl 4:9). For example, my wife and I have totally different personality types when it comes to planning and executing events, especially events for our church family. My wife wants to have a detailed plan of what we are going to do and tries to stick to the schedule and plan no matter what. On the other hand, I am more able and likely to go with the flow. We have learned how to work together to make the events we plan work well from the planning phase all the way through execution, even when things just won't go as planned. My wife is typically in charge of the planning and organizing, and then when the event happens, I take charge where I can adapt and make changes on the fly to help make the event a success. We learned the importance of working together because there were always issues when we tried to do things in only one of our preferred ways. However, when we learned to work together, we had greater success.

Conclusion

As Christian couples, we should all imitate the kind of ministry team partnership Aquila and Priscilla exemplified. Whenever Paul's writings address or mention this couple, he speaks not of two individuals, but of a couple so interconnected that to mention one is to mention the other. Their work is so closely tied together that they cannot be separated. This is the aspiration that all Christian couples should strive to attain. Let us be the kind of couples that emulate God's plan for marriage, to be helpers fit for each other, and so closely connected in our service that to mention one partner automatically includes the other.

Discussion Questions

1. Reflecting on Genesis 2:18, why do you think God emphasized the need for a "helper" for Adam, and how can this concept of complementary partnership strengthen a married couple's service in the church today?

2. Aquila and Priscilla worked together to support Paul, correct Apollos, and host a church in their home. What are some practical ways couples in our congregation can collaborate to support the church's mission, drawing from their example?

3. The lesson highlights how spouses with different strengths (e.g., planning vs. adaptability, emotional vs. logical approaches) can complement each other in ministry. Can you share an example of how you and your spouse (or a couple you know) have used your differences to serve the church more effectively?

4. Aquila and Priscilla's ministry was so unified that they were always mentioned together. How can married couples in our church cultivate such an interconnected partnership in serving God, and what challenges might they face in striving for this unity?

Endnotes

[1] All Scripture references are from the English Standard Version (ESV) unless otherwise specified.

[2] William Mounce. *Mounce's Complete Expository Dictionary of Old & New Testament Words*. (Grand Rapids: Zondervan, 2006), 332.

[3] Wenham, Gordon J. *Genesis*. Word Biblical Commentary Volume 1. (Dallas: Word Book, 1987).

Chapter 11

Like A Tree

Encouraging Each Other's Personal Growth

Keith Pickard

Focus Passages

Blessed is the man who walks not in the counsel of the wicked, nor stands in the way of sinners, nor sits in the seat of scoffers; but his delight is in the law of the LORD, and on his law he meditates day and night. He is like a tree planted by streams of water that yields its fruit in its season, and its leaf does not wither. In all that he does, he prospers (Ps 1:1–3).

Have this mind among yourselves, which is yours in Christ Jesus, who, though he was in the form of God, did not count equality with God a thing to be grasped, but emptied himself, by taking the form of a servant, being born in the likeness of men. And being found in human form, he humbled himself by becoming obedient to the point of death, even death on a cross. (Phil 2:5–8).[i]

One Main Thing

How sad it is for a couple in an unhappy marriage to say to one another, "I think we are growing apart." More than likely, the cause of two people growing apart is that they haven't been intentional about growing together. For marriage to succeed and become all that God has designed it to be, two people need to be committed to encouraging each other's personal growth. This is what we will be exploring in this chapter.

Introduction

While taking a trip to Washington, D.C. as a boy, I remember seeing the beautiful cherry blossoms in bloom. The gorgeous sight of hundreds of light pink trees impressed upon me the goodness and creativity of God. When we open the Scriptures, we see trees mentioned quite frequently. In biblical literature, trees illustrate life, health, and growth (Jer 17:7–8, Ezek 19:10, Num 24:5–6, Hos 14:5–8). The biblical authors use trees as symbols of righteous people who experience God's blessings (Ps 92:12–14, Prov 11:28). They flourish, prosper, and grow into something amazing like a tree planted by streams of water.

God desires our marriages to grow like trees—pictures of life, health, and flourishing (Eph 5:22–33). One of the ways that we maintain healthy and growing marriages is by becoming encouragers of each other. Everyone needs encouragement to reach their full potential. Timothy needed encouragement to live without fear (2 Tim 1:7). Philemon needed encouragement to take Onesimus back (Phlm 17–19). Peter needed encouragement to live without shame from past failures (John 21:15–19). Everyone needs encouragement, especially our spouses. When, like Jesus, we empty ourselves of selfishness and intentionally become each other's encouragers, we empower our marriages to become like flourishing trees planted by streams of water. Isn't this what we're all looking for? Let's dig deeper.

Going Deeper

If you want a tree to thrive, it must have the right environment. An apple tree would have a difficult time thriving in the middle of the Sahara Desert, and an orange tree probably wouldn't produce much fruit if it were in the Arctic. Nature (and sometimes gardeners) spreads seeds around seemingly at random, and sometimes one lands where it cannot possibly grow (cf. Luke 8:5–11). When planting wheat, this typically works out ok in the end. However, when planting a tree, especially one you wish to bear good fruit, you must also be intentional about placing it in the right environment. So it is with our marriages. Don't leave things to chance! Be intentional! We see this principle in Psalm 1:1–3:

> Blessed is the man who walks not in the counsel of the wicked, nor stands in the way of sinners, nor sits in the seat of scoffers; but his delight is in the law of the Lord, and on his law he meditates day and night. He is like a tree planted by streams of water that yields its fruit in its season, and its leaf does not wither. In all that he does, he prospers.

In the Psalm, the righteous man is likened to a tree. For the tree to grow, it must be in the right environment (being beside streams of water is especially helpful). At the same time, the righteous man must be in the right environment if he is going to grow. He must not walk under the counsel of the wicked, stand the way people who do evil do, or sit in company with those who are boastful and arrogant, but rather, he must immerse himself in God's word. God's word creates the right environment that will foster health, growth, and life. Righteous people must be intentional about keeping themselves in God's word (they must meditate on it, inviting it to be their primary source of delight). So, to be like a tree that flourishes, you need the right environment AND need to be intentional about creating and main-taining it.

There are principles here that apply to our discussion of marriage. To be effective encouragers of each other, we need to create the right environment AND be intentional about maintaining it. Jesus has created the right environ-ment for us to imitate. We see through His "mind" the kind of atmosphere that is suitable for growth:

> Have this mind among yourselves, which is yours in Christ Jesus, who, though he was in the form of God, did not count equality with God a thing to be grasped, but emptied himself, by taking the form of a servant, being born in the likeness of men. And being found in human form, he humbled himself by becoming obedient to the point of death, even death on a cross (Phil 2:5–8).

Though Jesus possessed power and glory as God of the world, He didn't use those things to trample over the weak and helpless. He descended to the status of a servant so that others could be blessed. Marriage should work the same way. Each spouse should descend from the mountaintops of pride into the valleys of humility, seeing themselves as servants of the other. This shapes the right environment that enables us to encourage our spouses to be everything the Lord has in mind. We must view ourselves as servants and embody the purpose of encouraging our spouses.

Additionally, we must be intentional about transmitting our attitude of growing unselfishness and humility into consistent actions. Jesus didn't end His work for us at the cross but continues to serve on our behalf as our merciful and faithful High Priest (Heb 7:24–25). Be a servant by showing interest in what your spouse values. When you show genuine interest in what your spouse is interested in, you communicate love and acceptance to them. You create an environment that encourages them to grow. Serve your spouse by identifying their talents and encouraging them to develop them (especially in service to the kingdom). Serve your husband or wife by delighting in God and meditating on His word, setting an example so that you both may grow spiritually.

Effective encouragement begins by learning from the tree in Psalm 1. Create the right environment of selflessness, like Jesus's, AND be intentional about embodying and demonstrating it through constant encouragement.

Application

- Adopt the servant mind of Jesus. As Christians, we are to "count others more significant than [ourselves]" (Phil 2:3). This is the kind of people we are called through Christ to be. We are people who love our neighbors like we love ourselves. One of the ways we apply this to our marriages is by making it our purpose to encourage the other. Even though it might be difficult sometimes, we need to adopt a servant identity toward our spouse, just like Jesus has toward us.

- Be interested in what interests your spouse. Dale Carnegie said, "To be interesting, be interested."[iii] Communicating to your spouse that you genuinely care about what interests them creates an atmosphere for the relationship to flourish and encourages their growth. Maybe your spouse has a hobby that you are not naturally inclined to like. Don't be afraid to get out of your comfort zone and do something with your spouse that they enjoy. Maybe they like to talk about sports, reading, or shared experiences. Show interest in what they are interested in, and you'll be communicating support and care.

- Affirm and encourage your spouse's talents and traits. Perhaps your spouse is a good conversationalist or has a great smile. Compliment your spouse on those positive qualities often. When your spouse displays Christ-like character by forgiving someone, or showing mercy, or being patient and gentle with a difficult person, let them know how proud you are of them for their example and love for Jesus. Affirm their talents and encourage them to take advantage of potential opportunities when they come. Identify the spiritual gifts you can see in your spouse and encourage them to use those gifts (Rom 12:3–8). They may not even be able to see their potential to serve Jesus if you don't first point it out. You serve your spouse like Jesus when you are committed to affirming them in their obedience to and imitation of Christ.

- Celebrate personal growth. If your spouse sets a weight loss goal, or finishes a degree, or gets a promotion at work, insist on celebrating it. Be vocal whenever they achieve something, and perhaps create a special occasion like a party or private dinner. Celebrating your spouse's accomplishments will encourage them to reach their full potential.

- Delight in God together. Read, study, and meditate on God's word as a couple. Conduct family worship regularly in your home. Initiate spiritual conversations while you are in the car or walking in the park. Delighting in God together in these ways will facilitate your personal and spiritual growth.

Conclusion

Blessed is the man who is like a tree! Blessed also is the couple who is like a tree! When we are committed to creating the right environment of selfless love and to being intentional about displaying that selflessness to our spouses, we will both surely be blessed.

Discussion Questions

1. What does it require of us to embrace a mind of selflessness like Jesus's in Philippians 2?

2. How do you think showing interest in what your spouse values encourages their personal growth?

3. What advantages are there in actively looking for and identifying the potential you see in your spouse?

4. Discuss creative ways that you could celebrate your spouse when they meet one of their goals.

5. How have you encouraged spiritual growth in your marriage in the past? How might you continue to encourage spiritual growth in marriage into the future?

6. What are some other ways that we can encourage each other's personal and spiritual growth?

Endnotes

[i] All Scripture references are from the English Standard Version (ESV) unless otherwise specified.

[ii] Dale Carnegie, *How to Win Friends and Influence People*, rev. ed. (New York: Simon and Schuster, 1981), 92.

Chapter 12

For Better or For Worse

How to Endure and Overcome Hardships Together

Shane Robinson

Focus Passage

> Through many tribulations we must enter the kingdom of God (Acts 14:22b).[i]

One Main Thing

Hardships in marriage and family are inevitable. Hardship, as defined in this lesson, is any difficulty, challenge, or suffering that tests a marriage or family's strength, unity, and faith. Hardships like poor financial decisions, lack of communication, and neglecting a spouse's emotional needs are avoidable. Yet, hardships like illness, infertility, job loss, or the loss of a loved one are often unavoidable. Avoidable hardships result from poor choices. Unavoidable hardships, on the other hand, are often beyond our control. How couples respond to and navigate obstacles determines whether they grow stronger or drift apart.

Introduction

I went to a marriage enrichment event with my wife several years ago. The event was in a hotel ballroom. There were about 500 people in attendance. Most of the couples were in their 20s and 30s. My wife and I were in our mid to late 30s and had been helped by attending these kinds of events in the past. The keynote speaker this particular year was a well-known "seasoned" preacher whom I'd heard preach a couple of times before. He was from my grandparents' generation, so I was eager to listen to what he had to say about marriage. His first words were, "I've been married over 60 years, and my wife and I have never once gotten into an argument." I waited for the punchline, but it never came. He was dead serious. I do not think he made the statement to boast, but I have no doubt he lost his audience within the first thirty seconds of his lesson.

Most marriages go through seasons of difficulty. Yet, as this section will argue, strong marriages are built by enduring through the hard times. Acts 14:22, while not addressing marriage, provides a principle for churches that couples would do well to understand—we will suffer many hardships. By looking at the circumstances in which Paul made this statement in Acts 14, we will notice practical ways to endure and overcome difficulties in marriage.

Going Deeper

Paul and Barnabas's first missionary journey sets the stage for our text. Their travels to Asia Minor aimed to preach the gospel and establish churches. A quick read through Acts 14 shows they faced opposition in each city they traveled through, but also gained converts. After escaping death in

Iconium (14:4–6) and Lystra (14:19), they went back to the same towns to "strengthen" and "exhort" the disciples (14:21–22). It is within this context that we read, "And when they had preached the gospel to that city and made many disciples, they returned to Lystra, Iconium, and Antioch, strengthening the souls of the disciples, exhorting them to continue in the faith, and saying, 'We must through many tribulations enter the kingdom of God'" (Acts 14:21–22 NKJV).

With this background in mind, we will notice some keywords and phrases used in Acts 14 that were *sources of adversity* for the church and apply them to marriage. Also, we will see some keywords and phrases used in Acts 14 that were *sources of hope* for the church to endure difficulties, and apply them to marriage as well.

Addressing Sources of Controversy

While this chapter may not address every source of controversy known to marriage, it does provide a few areas worthy of our attention. A small group of people caused trouble, creating much of the controversy. This minority group was effective in turning the majority against the apostles by "poisoning" their minds (14:2) and "persuading" people to believe something that was not true (14:19).

After making commitments "for better or for worse," newlywed couples usually face the "worse" before they enjoy the "better." While disputes often arise due to a lack of quality time, sex, money, etc., many difficulties arise in the early years of marriage due to outside influences. These "outside influences" may be parents, in-laws, friends, coworkers, or "influencers" on social media. While these influences may not intend to harm a marriage, they often create conflict and controversy.

Similar to how we can read through Acts 14 and identify potential causes of controversy, it is also helpful to take inventory of our lives to pinpoint people, places, and things that confuse or "poison" our relationships. If you can identify sources of controversy that are harmful to your marriage, and you want "for better," you may do well to avoid them for a season and focus on strengthening your relationship with your spouse.

Addressing Sources of Hope

After being run out of town, stoned, and left for dead, Paul went back to see the brethren in the same cities where he faced persecution (14:21). His purpose, according to Luke, was to "strengthen" and "exhort" the disciples. Paul wanted the brethren to find strength physically, emotionally, relationally, and spiritually. Furthermore, he wanted them to be consoled and encouraged to know that their labor in the kingdom throughout hard times would pay off.

Every relationship needs to be "strengthened" and "encouraged." When discouragement, negativity, lack of trust, or lack of mutual support fill a relationship, spouses can feel neglected, betrayed, and misunderstood. While different seasons of marriage consume different levels of time and energy, communication, quality time, and words of appreciation require continuous intentionality and effort. Healthy and stable relationships do not flourish by accident.

Think about the look on the brethren's faces when Paul and Barnabas came back into town. These men who had risked their lives for the gospel are now back in town out of love and concern for the brethren. Their presence was a testimony to God's work in their lives. Their message testified to the reality that life is hard, and we must take incredible risks to strengthen our relationships for the kingdom's sake. In marriage, the time we invest in others says much about our care and concern. When we take risks to strengthen and encourage those closest to us, we demonstrate Christ's love by prioritizing others' needs above our own (Phil 2:1–5).

Application

- *Put some distance between outside influences that hurt your marriage.* Outside influences can "poison" a healthy marriage. For some couples, this may mean putting distance between themselves and extended family. For others, it may mean limiting time on social media. One of the best decisions I made early on in marriage was to move out of town for a few years to work on my career. While I do not believe any of those relationships were out to harm my marriage, I do admit they caused confusion and conflict. Looking back, I could focus on my family without being influenced by my parents, in-laws, or friends. The distance between specific outside influences strengthened my marriage.
- *Couples who endure serve as examples for couples needing endurance.* Marriage takes a considerable amount of energy. Times can and will be hard. Many marriages in need of endurance, sadly, end in divorce. On the other

hand, some marriages endure through "much tribulation" and are much better as a result. These marriages become living testimonies to others walking through their struggles. If your marriage is struggling, look to other couples who've "endured" financial hardships, health crises, parenting challenges, or whatever your marriage is struggling through. Take the successful couple out to dinner, share your struggles, and ask for advice. Allow their endurance to serve as a source of encouragement through whatever season of life you find yourself in. If you have remained faithful to your vows and endured hardship, stay the course and inspire others to fight for their marriages rather than give up. Mentor younger couples.

Conclusion

Whether you are going through a season of difficulty, just coming through a season of difficulty, or about to face a season of difficulty, recognize that hardships in marriage are inevitable. Every marriage experiences trials. The marriages that grow stronger and wiser have not done so without enduring challenges in life. Seasons of hardship will come and go. Generally, the more effort couples put into their marriage in the beginning, the better off it will be.

Difficulties in marriage are often seasonal. To illustrate, sleepless nights with a newborn, financial strain in the early years, or the growing pains of parenting teens usually only last a few years. Instead of seeing hardships as obstacles, view them as opportunities to grow in love, strengthen your faith, and build a marriage that not only lasts but thrives. Just as Paul and Barnabas encouraged the early disciples to persevere through trials, we must encourage one another to remain steadfast in our marriages.

Discussion Questions

1. How can outside influences, such as family, friends, or social media, create tension in a marriage?

2. What are some struggles in marriage that are avoidable? Would you say these struggles result from poor choices or behaviors? Why or why not?

3. What are some unavoidable hardships associated with marriage or family life? What about these hardships was beyond a couple's control?

4. What does the Bible teach about enduring trials in relationships? How can passages like Acts 14:22, Romans 5:3–5, or James 1:2–4 shape our understanding of hardships in marriage?

5. Can you think of a time when you or someone you know faced a hardship in marriage? What helped or hurt the situation?

Endnotes

[i] All Scripture references are from the English Standard Version (ESV) unless otherwise specified.

Chapter 13

Until Death Do Us Part

Learning to Forgive as Christ Forgives
Brandon Beard

Focus Passage

But that is not the way you learned Christ!—assuming that you have heard about him and were taught in him, as the truth is in Jesus, to put off your old self, which belongs to your former manner of life and is corrupt through deceitful desires, and to be renewed in the spirit of your minds, and to put on the new self, created after the likeness of God in true righteousness and holiness.

Therefore, having put away falsehood, let each one of you speak the truth with his neighbor, for we are members one of another. Be angry and do not sin; do not let the sun go down on your anger, and give no opportunity to the devil. Let the thief no longer steal, but rather let him labor, doing honest work with his own hands, so that he may have something to share with anyone in need. Let no corrupting talk come out of your mouths, but only such as is good for building up, as fits the occasion, that it may give grace to those who hear. And do not grieve the Holy

Spirit of God, by whom you were sealed for the day of redemption. Let all bitterness and wrath and anger and clamor and slander be put away from you, along with all malice. Be kind to one another, tenderhearted, forgiving one another, as God in Christ forgave you.

Therefore be imitators of God, as beloved children. And walk in love, as Christ loved us and gave himself up for us, a fragrant offering and sacrifice to God (Eph 4:20–5:2).[1]

One Main Thing

One of the Bible words in the original languages, often translated as "forgive" (Greek: "*aphiemi*"), is also sometimes translated as "divorce." The root meaning of *aphiemi* is to "let go, send away." Paul uses this word three times in 1 Corinthians 7:11–13 to mean "to send away your spouse." Yet in Luke 11:4 and John 20:23, this same word is shaped by context to mean "the releasing or letting go of sin." If we are committed to preserving our marriages, resisting the notion of "letting go," we must consider that we are instead called to "release from guilt." The wordplay is brilliant. Scripture teaches husbands and wives not to divorce each other, but to "divorce" themselves from holding a grudge over repented sins. Consider what hurts you that you must "put away" to ensure you are never tempted to "put away" your spouse!

Introduction

We are either growing to become more and more like Christ or drifting further from His likeness and falling back into the sinful ways of the world. Scripture does not offer us a "happy middle" ground. There's no such thing as lasting happiness in the context of unrepentant sin. Whether it is the lukewarm idea in Revelation 3 or Paul's exhortation to the Romans not to be lazy with zeal, we all have work to do, including in our marriages.

Nothing will mature a Christian faster than living with a spouse striving to be more like Christ every day. You can't think that, just because we are Christians and have put on Christ in baptism (Gal 3:27), that we are permitted to lose the drive to be more like Him every day that led us into the water as an act of faith to begin with. Too many believers give up when things get difficult, but the promise of Galatians 6:9 assures us that's the wrong thing to do. The old cultural proverb says, "All good things come to those who wait." That's true, as long as the waiting means enduring the hard work to reap the benefit. It is worth it to stick it out through difficult seasons in marriage. Live with a stubborn "the best is yet to come" mentality.

Going Deeper

Paul exhorts the Ephesians (and all believers) to abandon various detrimental behaviors and attitudes. He instructs them to forsake their former selves, falsehood, anger, unwholesome speech, bitterness, and impure desires. His rationale is rooted in their calling to a renewed life in Christ (4:24), which emulates His sacrificial love (5:1–2). Retaining the detrimental traits grieves the Holy Spirit (4:30) and undermines our relationships that God intends to bless us and produce flourishing.

As mentioned above, the original Greek term, *aphiemi*, illuminates this. In 1 Corinthians 7, it refers to divorce, the sending away of a spouse, while in Luke and John, it signifies the forgiveness of sin. To maintain the integrity of marriage, we must release what threatens it. Let us examine this through a series of five daily considerations.

Consideration 1: Relinquishing the former self.

Paul instructs, "Put off your old self, which belongs to your former manner of life and is corrupt through deceitful desires" (4:22). The old nature—characterized by selfishness and pride—persists in its attempts to resurface in us as long as we live in this fallen world. Break old habits by replacing them with wholesome ones. Blaze new pathways of travel that steer you away from former pitfalls. "Be careful little eyes, hands, feet," etc. Do not nurture bitter, selfish thought patterns. Learn to listen to what you are saying to yourself and steer that inner dialogue in biblical directions. How often should you relinquish your former, sinful self? Every day.

Consideration 2: Abandon Falsehood.

"Put off falsehood and speak truthfully to your neighbor" (4:25). Truthfulness is the bedrock of trust, yet deceit, whether overt or subtle, can infiltrate even the strongest relationships. On one occasion, I offered a dismissive "I am well" when I was deeply inwardly burdened, only to find that this evasion led to further complications. Honesty, though sometimes difficult, fosters clarity and connection. Past secrets, if concealed, fester. Present untruths breed misunderstanding. Daily abandonment of falsehood ensures a marriage grounded in authenticity and mutual reliance. How often should you abandon falsehood? Every day.

Consideration 3: Forsake Unwholesome Speech.

"Nor should there be obscenity, foolish talk or coarse joking, which are out of place" (5:4). Paul identifies such language as incompatible with the believer's calling, advocating instead for expressions of gratitude. I have, at times, allowed careless words or ill-timed jests to escape my lips, only to witness to my sorrow their unintended negative impact on my spouse. Forsaking these daily and replacing them with encouragement restores dignity to our interactions. It heals lingering hurts, maintains present harmony, and prevents future discord, manifesting the holiness to which we are called. How often should you forsake unwholesome speech, including obscene, foolish talk, and coarse joking? Every day.

Consideration 4: Release Anger.

"Be angry and do not sin; do not let the sun go down on your anger, and give no opportunity to the devil" (4:26–27). Anger, when left unresolved, becomes a barrier to intimacy. Recently, a disagreement regarding family responsibilities stirred frustration within me, yet adherence to Paul's counsel prompted a resolution before nightfall. Releasing anger daily prevents it from accumulating, whether from past offenses or present conflicts. Failure to do so, Paul warns, grants opportunity to the adversary (4:27). By consistently letting it go, we preserve the unity and peace essential to marital fidelity. How often should you release anger? Every day.

In his book, *Unoffendable*, Brant Hansen writes,

We should forfeit our right to be offended. That means forfeiting our right to hold on to anger. When we do this, we'll be making a sacrifice that's very pleasing to God. It strikes at our very pride. It forces us not only to think about humility but to actually be humble. I used to think it was incumbent upon a Christian to take offense. I now believe we should be the most refreshingly unoffendable people on a planet that seems to spin on an axis of offense. [2]

Consideration 5: Affirm Love to Your Spouse.

Paul emphasizes edification (encouraging words that uplift rather than diminish) in Ephesians 4:29. Verbal affirmations of love are vital to strengthening the marital bond. The blessed one in Psalm 1, meditating daily, frequently hears the Father's "I love you." Imitate this toward your spouse (Eph 5:1). Give them something true, beautiful, and good to nourish their souls.

There was a time when, amidst the demands of work and family, I neglected to express my love to my wife for several days at a time. The absence of that needed reassurance was felt, creating a subtle distance between us. Affirming love daily—through words *and* actions—mends past wounds, fortifies present unity, and establishes a foundation of trust for the future. It is a deliberate act that counters the drift that neglect might otherwise permit. How frequently should you express love to your spouse? Every day.

Application

"Bitterness is a liar."[3] If I tell a lie about you and later you confront me about it or my conscience convicts me, do I feel guilty or bitter? In most cases, the answer is guilty. I messed up and need forgiveness. Now, if you tell a lie about me and spread it around, am I more apt to feel guilty or bitter? Most likely, bitter. You are attempting to hurt me somehow, and I do not appreciate it. So, the conclusion must be as follows. Guilt is when I sin, and bitterness is when you sin. Right? Think again! Guilt is when I sin, and bitterness is when I sin. That's the truth! How often must Christian husbands and wives deal with guilt and bitterness to avoid poisoning the marriage? Yes. Every day!

Whether mastering a skill like chess, running a marathon, preaching a sermon, or climbing the corporate ladder, making measurable progress in a reasonable time is the name of the game. The same goes for the whole Christian race (1 Cor 9:24–26, Gal 5:7). Nurturing healthy, God-honoring marriages is very much a part of the Christian race to the glorious finish. Maybe your marriage needs a kickstart to renew these Ephesians 4:20–5:2 admonitions. Perhaps it needs a restart. In any case, it only takes one *to* start. Whether it's a start or a restart, decide right now to start making measurable progress in a reasonable time. Forgive, that you may be forgiven (Matt 6:14–15; Luke 6:37, 11:4).

Conclusion

It's Sunday afternoon, and I am at the church building when one of my kids barges into my office excitedly, asking me, "Dad, are you going to do Kingdom Kids?" Fifteen minutes before church service begins on Sunday nights, our young kids come together for what we call Kingdom Kids. It is an enjoyable time to get the little ones together and have them memorize Bible facts and principles that we all hope will stick with them as they grow. No matter the main topic, we always ask the same four questions within those moments before they all find their seats in the auditorium. Those questions are: (1) What is the definition of a successful life? —To live your life and go to Heaven. (2) What is the definition of an unsuccessful life? —To live your life and not go to Heaven. (3) What is God's plan for marriage? —One man and one woman for life. (4) When you grow up, who will you marry if you choose to get married? —A Christian.

The answer to those last two questions goes much deeper than a surface-level understanding of God's plan for marriage. Ephesians 4:20–5:2 isn't just theology—it's a call to measurable progress. If we would succeed in keeping our marriage vow, "Until death do us part," it will take forgiveness, maybe a lot of it, so do it. Forgive.

Discussion Questions

1. What past hurts have you struggled to let go of in your marriage? How can you start forgiving them?
2. How do you handle present hurts with your spouse? What's one way you could extend grace this week?
3. What's one thing you need to put away to avoid future hurts? How will you do it?
4. How does daily forgiveness change the way you see your marriage?

5. Why does God's plan for the permanency of forgiveness matter, and how can you live it out every day?

Endnotes

[1] All Scripture references are from the English Standard Version (ESV) unless otherwise specified.

[2] Brant Hansen, *Unoffendable: How Just One Change Can Make All of Life Better*, updated ed. (Nashville: Thomas Nelson, 2023).

[3] I first heard this concept from the late Jim Wilson in a YouTube video.

Scripture Index

Old Testament
Genesis

Meet the Contributing Authors

Joshua Pappas serves as the Preaching Minister for LaVergne Church of Christ in LaVergne, TN. He is a graduate of Heritage Christian University with a B.A. and M.Min. degrees. He has been married to his High School sweetheart, Keshia, for 28 years. They have two grown sons, Nathan and Logan, both faithful followers of Jesus, a daughter-in-law, and a beloved grandson, hopefully the first of many. Josh has conducted church leadership, discipleship, education, and marriage seminars and workshops in several churches and preaches by appointment in lectureships, summer series, and gospel meetings. He is one of the hosts of the Conversion Conversation Podcast. Contact him at pappy1975@gmail.com.

Marricus Ellis serves as the Senior Minister at Bouldercrest Church of Christ in Atlanta, GA. He studied at the Nashville School of Preaching and earned his B.A. in Biblical Studies and is currently pursuing his M.Div. from Heritage Christian University. He is married to Jamila Ellis, and they have one son named Judah. Marricus Ellis preaches at gospel meetings and conferences throughout the brotherhood. He also enjoys hosting a podcast, The Lamp and Light Podcast, where he encourages individuals to allow God's word to lead and guide their daily lives. Contact Marricus at marricus@bouldercrestcoc.org.

Matthew Morine serves as the Pulpit Minister for the Castle Rock Church of Christ in Castle Rock, CO. He earned his B.A. from Heritage Christian University, his M.A. In Biblical Studies from Lipscomb University, his M.Div. from Freed-Hardeman University, and his D.Min. from Harding Graduate School of Religion. Matthew has been married to Charity for 23 years, and they have two children: Gabrielle, who is in college, and Noah, who is a senior in high school. Matthew does workshops on Natural Evangelism and workshops for discipleship called Wild Transformation, and has spoken in lectureships and youth events. Contact Matthew at mmorine@hotmail.com.

Chris Miller preaches for the Hatton Church of Christ in Town Creek, AL. He earned B.A. and M.A. degrees from Heritage Christian University. Christ and his wife, Skye, have three children. Chris preaches in gospel meetings, lectureships, and youth events. Contact Chris at hattoncoc@yahoo.com.

Jon Hackett serves as Pulpit Minister for the Lomax Church of Christ in Hohenwald, TN. He earned his B.A. in Mass Communications from the University of South Alabama and his M.A. in Organizational Development with a Graduate Certificate in Conflict Resolution, Reconciliation, and Mediation from Abilene Christian University. He has been married to Rachel Fetner Hackett for 29 years, and they have two adult daughters, Emily and Catherine. He preaches in meetings and speaks at youth and adult events, leads and facilitates various workshops and seminars on topics like Marriage and Family, Leadership Training, Organizational Development, and Conflict Resolution, for churches, organizations, and businesses. He also leads groups of people who are interested in doing short-term mission trips to Kenya and/or pilgrimages to Greece and Israel to walk in the footsteps of those in the Bible.

Jerrie Barber serves congregations as an interim minister and has served numerous churches very well in this capacity. He presently serves the Hartsville Pike congregation in Gallatin, TN. He previously served congregations in Georgia, Kentucky, and Tennessee over a 50-year preaching career. He earned his Third Year Certificate in Bible from Freed-Hardeman University and his B.A. from Lipscomb University. He has been married to Gail Champion Barber for 60 years. They have two children, Jerrie Wayne, II, and Christi Parsons, six grandchildren, and five great-grandchildren. Jerrie writes two blogs, New Shepherds Orientation: www.newshepherdsorientation.com and Between Preachers: www.betweenpreachers.com. He also has a podcast, called Gleaning Mustard Seeds: https://www.buzzsprout.com/2369804. Jerrie has led 26 sessions of the New Shepherds Orientation Workshop, a weekend seminar for elders, preachers, and spouses. Contact Jerrie at jerrie@barberclippings.com.

Evan Kirby has been utterly privileged to be married to Kristin for 14 years and has been blessed beyond measure with three wonderful daughters named Ella, Lydia, and Iris. Evan and Kristin reside in LaGrange, GA, where they both labor with the Broad Street Church of Christ, Evan working as the preaching minister and Kristin as the children's minister. Evan has a B.A. in Biblical Studies and a M.Min. in Ministerial Counseling from Heritage Christian University. He loves to speak about the historical spiritual disciplines as they aid us in keeping in step with the Spirit on the path of discipleship with Jesus. Contact him at erkirby15@gmail.com.

Jacob Rutledge serves the Dripping Springs Church of Christ as Preaching Minister. He earned his B.A. in Bible from Heritage Christian University as well as his M.S. in Ministry from Amridge University. He has been married to Jessica for 15 years, and they have three children, Natalie, Easton, and Lincoln.

Matthew Thigpen serves as the Minister for the Fulton Church of Christ in Fulton, MS. He earned A.A., B.A., and M.A. degrees in Bible and New Testament from Heritage Christian University, and his M.Div. from Freed-Hardeman University. Matthew and his wife Paula have one daughter, Elizabeth, and one son, Austin. He accepts appointments to preach in gospel meetings and other speaking engagements. Contact him at matthewthig@hotmail.com.

Keith Pickard is the Preaching Minister for the Bethel Church of Christ in Dunlap, TN. He earned his B.S. in Bible from Freed-Hardeman University and his M.Div. from Heritage Christian University. He has been married to Anna for 7 years, and they have 2 children, Titus and Alison. Alongside his local work, Keith enjoys preaching in gospel meetings. Contact him at kpickard0793@gmail.com.

Shane Robinson is the Preaching Minister for Central Church of Christ in Dalton, GA. He has been in full-time ministry for 20 years and is presently working towards a degree in Social work. He has been married to his wife, Jennifer, for 22 years, and they have four children at home. Shane is committed to helping people realize their value in Christ and potential in His kingdom and is available to speak in churches by appointment. Contact him at shane@ccocdalton.org

Brandon Beard serves as Family and Outreach Minister for the Dewey Church of Christ in Dewey, OK. He earned his B.A. in Biblical Studies from Heritage Christian University. He and his wife Kelsy have been married for 13 years, and have two children, Nora and Jack. Brandon likes to point people to resources that will help them learn and grow. Contact him at theamazingb@gmail.com for suggestions about resources (books, videos, etc.) on just about anything to do with life and godliness, mental health, productivity, apologetics, etc.

Jesus Loves Families Series

Concerned about the families in your congregation? Want to improve your family? The Jesus Loves Families series, published by Heritage Christian University's Cypress Publications, equips Christian couples with Bible-based teaching to strengthen their marriages and raise faithful children. Every healthy, growing congregation needs to offer continual instruction and encouragement to its member families. This series provides reliable material to meet this need. The series will include four volumes. Volume one provides 13 chapters on the biblical foundations of marriage and family. Volume two will focus on parenting young children from birth to pre-teen. Volume three will address parenting teens and young adults transitioning to independence. Volume four will tackle contemporary challenges, guiding parents to protect their children from worldly influences, nurture their faith, and raise them as bold disciples of Christ. Readers will find the diversity of style and expression of the contributing authors refreshing. Those who love the Bible will appreciate the respect for God's word as both relevant and authoritative. Each volume in this series is intended for individual and group Bible study.

CYPRESS

To see full catalog of Heritage Christian University Press
and its imprint Cypress Publications, visit
www.hcu.edu/publications